English Brushup

Fifth Edition

John Langan
Atlantic Cape Community College

Janet M. Goldstein

Mc
Graw
Hill

Connect
Learn
Succeed™

The McGraw-Hill Companies

Connect
Learn
Succeed™

Published by McGraw-Hill, an imprint of The McGraw-Hill Companies, Inc., 1221 Avenue of the Americas, New York, NY 10020. Copyright © 2011. All rights reserved. No part of this publication may be reproduced or distributed in any form or by any means, or stored in a database or retrieval system, without the prior written consent of The McGraw-Hill Companies, Inc., including, but not limited to, in any network or other electronic storage or transmission, or broadcast for distance learning.

This book is printed on acid-free paper.

2 3 4 5 6 7 8 9 DOC/DOC 1 5 4 3 2 1

ISBN-13 (Student Edition):   978-0-07-742836-5
ISBN-10 (Student Edition):   0-07-742836-6
ISBN-13 (Instructor's Edition):   978-0-07-742837-2
ISBN-10 (Instructor's Edition):   0-07-742837-4

Vice President, Editorial: *Michael Ryan*
Publisher: *David Patterson*
Sponsoring Editor: *John Kindler*
Editorial Coordinator: *Jesse Hassenger*
Marketing Manager: *Jaclyn Elkins*
Developmental Editor: *Nomi Sofer*
Project Manager: *Jasmin Tokatlian*
Designer: *Preston Thomas*
Cover Illustration: *Paul Turnbaugh and Judith Ogus*
Media Project Manager: *Bethuel Jabez*
Production Supervisor: *Tandra Jorgensen*
Composition: *11/13 Times Roman by Laserwords Private Limited*
Printing: *45# New Era Matte Plus, R.R. Donnelley & Sons*

Library of Congress Cataloging-in-Publication Data

Langan, John.
   English brushup / John Langan, Janet M. Goldstein.—5th ed.
      p. cm.
   Includes index.
   ISBN-13: 978-0-07-742836-5 (student ed. : acid-free paper)
   ISBN-10: 0-07-742836-6 (student ed. : acid-free paper)
   ISBN-13: 978-0-07-742837-2 (annotated instructor's ed. : acid-free paper)
   ISBN-10: 0-07-742837-4 (annotated instructor's ed. : acid-free paper)
      1. English language—Rhetoric—Problems, exercises, etc. 2. English language—Grammar—Problems, exercises, etc. I. Goldstein, Janet M. II. Title.

PE1413.L28 2010
428.2—dc22

                                                              2009028589

The Internet addresses listed in the text were accurate at the time of publication. The inclusion of a Web site does not indicate an endorsement by the authors or McGraw-Hill, and McGraw-Hill does not guarantee the accuracy of the information presented at these sites.

www.mhhe.com

Contents

Part Two: Extending the Skills   183

Part Three: Applying the Skills   229

To the Instructor

English Brushup is a quick and practical guide to the grammar, punctuation, and usage skills that students most need to know. The book contains features that distinguish it from other grammar texts on the market:

1 *Three-part format.* In order to highlight the most vital skills, the book is divided into three parts. Part One presents primary information about sixteen key skills. Part Two includes secondary information about these skills and also covers topics not discussed in Part One. Part Three tests students' mastery of the skills taught in Part One.

2 *Self-teaching approach.* The *first page of every chapter* in Part One begins with an informal test—and then provides the answers and explanations. Students can quickly see what they know and don't know about the skill in question. In some cases, they may learn what they need to know about the skill without going any further in the chapter.

The *next three to five pages* of each chapter present the basics about the skill. Lively examples and brief exercises give students the chance to practice the grammatical principle involved. Answers at the back of the book allow students to correct their own work, teaching themselves as they go.

The *last six pages of each chapter* consist of six tests on the skill. Half of the items in Tests 1, 3, and 5 are accompanied by *hints*—shown in a second color—which are designed to guide students in thinking through each kind of correction. More self-teaching is therefore ensured.

In addition, as students work through the tests, they master the skills in progressively longer passages. In Tests 1 and 2, students practice the skills in sentences; in Tests 3 and 4, they work with short passages; finally, in Tests 5 and 6, they apply the skills to entire paragraphs. Step by step, then, their mastery of the skills advances from the sentence to the paragraph level.

3 *Manageable size.* The book's compact size and short chapters will not overwhelm students. In addition, *English Brushup* does not discourage or confuse students by offering an equal amount of coverage for every grammar rule. Instead, Part One of the book presents only those rules that students actually *need to know* to write well. Additional useful information about many skills appears in Part Two.

4 *Invaluable supplements.* An *Instructor's Edition* consists of the student text, as well as answers to all the practices and tests. An *Instructor's Manual and Test Bank,* one of several resources available online for instructors at

http://www.mhhe.com/langan, contains a diagnostic test and an achievement test as well as four additional mastery tests for each of the skills in Part One of the book. To provide for a range of student needs, the first two tests are relatively easy, and the second two are more difficult.

Other features of the book include the following:

- Simple language rather than traditional grammatical terminology.
- Examples and practice materials that are "real-life," high-interest, sometimes amusing, and always *adult*.
- An insistence that students play an active role in the learning process, not just "correcting," as in so many grammar books, but actually *writing out* corrections.

In short, *English Brushup* offers a combination of appealing features not found in other texts. Its focus on important skills, self-teaching approach, reasonable size, and outstanding supplements may prompt you to decide that *English Brushup* is the grammar book best suited to the needs of today's students.

Changes in the Fifth Edition

- "Parts of Speech" has been moved to the Introduction, where it will prepare students for the grammar skills covered in Part One.
- In Part Two, each chapter now begins on its own page, and a new chapter, "Mixed Constructions," has been added.
- Two new Combined Mastery Tests have been added to Part Three, and practice materials and tests have been freshened throughout the book.

Acknowledgments

Reviewers who have provided helpful suggestions for this edition include Kristin Brunnemer, Pierce College; Michael Darcher, Pierce College; Patricia Drown, Southwest Minnesota State University; Susan Ertel, Dixie State College of Utah; Elizabeth Langenfeld, Crafton Hills College; Robin Lowe, Itawamba Community College; Anna Maheshwari, Schoolcraft College; Allison Martin, Bossier Parish Community College; Thomas Nicholas, Lansing Community College; and Lida Jane Strot, Minneapolis Community and Technical College.

We also owe thanks to Fran Hamilton, for providing additional practice materials for this edition, and to John Kindler, Nomi Sofer, and Jasmin Tokatlian at McGraw-Hill.

John Langan
Janet M. Goldstein

Introduction

WHY BRUSH UP YOUR ENGLISH?

Suppose you saw the following sign in a convenience store:

- Please dont put children in our shopping carts, they are unstable. And can fall over easily.

... or read the following line in a student's history paper:

- The soldiers in the civil war often weared rags, on there feet that were torn from scraps of old clothing.

... or read the following sentence in a business memo:

- Profit's at the company has doubled in the passed 3 months its been our best sales performance in several yrs.

... or read the following paragraph in a job application:

- This June I will graduate. With twenty-four hours of courses in accounting. I have alot of previous experience. One was as a clerk in the school bookstore, the other doing data entry for ryder truck rental.

Chances are that the writers of the above lines felt vaguely uneasy about their sentences. They may have had doubts about whether their English was correct and clear. However, they went ahead because their work or school situation required them to put words on paper.

Here is what the four writers above should have written:

- Please don't put children in our shopping carts. The carts are unstable and can fall over easily.

- On their feet, the soldiers in the Civil War often wore rags that were torn from scraps of old clothing.

- Profits at the company have doubled in the past three months. It's been our best sales performance in several years.

- This June I will graduate with twenty-four hours of courses in accounting. I have a lot of previous experience. One position I have held was as a clerk in the school bookstore; the other was doing data entry for Ryder Truck Rental.

If you were uncertain about the corrections needed for the above sentences, then this book is for you. *English Brushup* is a guide to the essentials of English: the grammar, punctuation, and usage skills that you most need to write clearly and effectively.

HOW *ENGLISH BRUSHUP* WORKS

Here is one way to use the book:

1 **Look at the table of contents.** You'll see that *English Brushup* is divided into three parts. Part One presents sixteen key skills you need in order to write well. Part Two includes more information about some of the skills in Part One; it also covers some areas not included in Part One. Part Three contains a series of tests you can take after you have studied the skills in Part One.

2 **Turn to the first page of any chapter in Part One.** Take the "Seeing What You Know" test. Then check your answers. If you have a problem with the skill, you'll know it right away. In some cases, you may learn what you need to know about the skill without going any further in the chapter.

3 **Work through the rest of the chapter.** The next three to five pages of each chapter present the basics of the skill. The examples and brief exercises will give you the chance to practice the skill. The answers at the back of the book will allow you to correct your own work, teaching yourself as you go.

4 **Test yourself.** The last six pages of each chapter contain six tests on the skill. Tests 1, 3, and 5 usually include hints that will help you understand and answer half of the items on the tests. Be sure to take advantage of these hints to increase your mastery of the skill. You will find additional tests in Part Three, "Applying the Skills."

5 **Use the book as a reference tool.** Following the above sequence, work your way through the book. In Part Two, pay special attention to the section on paper format on pages 185–186. Refer to other sections of Part Two as needed or as your instructor suggests. To help you find your way around the book, use the table of contents at the front, the index at the back, and the correction symbols and page references on the inside front cover.

AN INTRODUCTION TO GRAMMAR: THE PARTS OF SPEECH

Parts of speech are classifications of words according to their meaning and use in a sentence. There are eight parts of speech:

nouns	verbs	adjectives	conjunctions
pronouns	prepositions	adverbs	interjections

Part One

Sixteen Basic Skills

Preview

Part One presents basic information about sixteen key grammar, punctuation, and usage skills:

1 Subjects and Verbs

Seeing What You Know

In each blank, insert a word that seems appropriate. Then read the explanations below.

1. The _____ accidentally _____ onto the floor.

2. My _____ often _____ at the mail carrier.

3. A _____ in the corner _____ loudly to the waitress.

4. _____ should never have _____ to study all night for the test.

Understanding the Answers

If your completed sentences make grammatical sense, the word in the first blank of each sentence will be its **subject**, and the word in the second blank will be the **verb**. Here are some completed versions of the sentences, with the subjects and verbs labeled:

1. The **knife** *(subject)* accidentally **fell** *(verb)* onto the floor.
   The *knife* is what the sentence is about. *Fell* is what the knife did.

2. My **cat** *(subject)* often **meows** *(verb)* at the mail carrier.
   The *cat* is the one the sentence is about. *Meows* is what the cat does.

3. A **customer** *(subject)* in the corner **shouted** *(verb)* loudly to the waitress.
   A *customer* is performing an action. *Shouted* is the action.

4. **Anita** *(subject)* **should** never **have tried** *(verb)* to study all night for the test.
   Anita is the person doing something. *Should [never] have tried* is what the sentence says about her. *Never* is not part of the verb.

Subjects and verbs are the basic parts of sentences. Understanding them will help you with most of the other skills in this book.

FINDING THE SUBJECT

Look at the following sentences:

Eric tripped on the steps.

The brakes on my car squeal.

She owns three motorcycles.

Depression is a common mood disorder.

The **subject** of a sentence is the person, thing, or idea that the sentence is about. To find a sentence's subject, ask yourself, "Who or what is this sentence about?" or "Who or what is doing something in this sentence?"*

Let's look again at the sentences above.

Who is the first one about? *Eric.* (He's the one who tripped.)

What is the second one about? *Brakes.* (They are what squeal.)

Who is the third one about? *She.* (She's the one who owns three motorcycles.)

What is the fourth one about? *Depression.* (It's a common mood disorder.)

So, in the sentences above, the subjects are *Eric, brakes, she,* and *depression.*

Note   Each of these subjects is either a **noun** (the name of a person, place, or thing) or a **pronoun** (a word that stands for a noun). The subject of a sentence will always be either a noun or a pronoun. For more information about nouns and pronouns, see pages 81–84.

The Subject Is Never in a Prepositional Phrase

The subject of a sentence will never be part of a prepositional phrase. A **prepositional phrase**, such as *on my car,* is a group of words that begins with a preposition, ends with a noun or pronoun (the object of the preposition), and answers a question such as "Which one?" "What kind?" "How?" "Where?" or "When?"

Here are some common prepositions:

Prepositions					
about	around	beside	for	off	under
above	at	between	from	on, onto	until
across	before	by	in, into	over	up
after	behind	down	inside	through	upon
along	below	during	like	to	with
among	beneath	except	of	toward	without

---

*In imperative sentences (commands), the subject is understood to be *you:* [You] Come here. [You] Please bring me the check. [You] Stop snoring!

As you look for the subject of a sentence, it is helpful to cross out any prepositional phrases that you find.

The vase ~~on the bedside table~~ belonged ~~to my grandparents~~. (*Vase* is the subject; *on the bedside table* is a prepositional phrase telling us which vase.)

~~With smiles or frowns~~, students left the exam room. (*Students* is the subject; *with smiles or frowns* is a prepositional phrase describing how they left.)

The noise ~~during the thunderstorm~~ was frightening. (*Noise* is the subject; *during the thunderstorm* is a prepositional phrase telling when it happened.)

FINDING THE VERB

The subject of a sentence is what that sentence is about. The **verb** explains what that sentence says about the subject. Consider the four sentences on the previous page:

What does the first sentence say about Eric? He *tripped.*

What does the second sentence say about the brakes? They *squeal.*

What does the third sentence say about the woman? She *owns* (three motorcycles).

What does the last sentence say about depression? It *is* (a mood disorder).

The verbs in the sentences above are *tripped, squeal, owns,* and *is.*
Here are two other ways to identify a verb:

1   Try putting a pronoun such as *I, you, he, she, it,* or *they* in front of it. If the word is a verb, the resulting sentence will make sense. Notice that in the examples above, *he tripped, they squeal, she owns,* and *it is* all make sense.

2   Look at what the verb tells us. Most verbs show action; they are called **action verbs**. (*Tripped, owns,* and *squeal* are action verbs.) A few verbs, however, are **linking verbs**. They link (join) the subject to something that is said about the subject. In the fourth example, *is* is a linking verb. It connects the subject, *depression,* with an idea about depression (it is a *common mood disorder*). *Am, are, was, were, look, feel, sound, appear, seem, grow, remain,* and *become* are other common linking verbs.

Practice 1

In each of the sentences below, cross out the prepositional phrases. Then underline the subject once and the verb twice. The first one is done for you as an example.

1. <u>Nikki</u> <u><u>waited</u></u> ~~in the supermarket checkout line for nearly half an hour~~.

2.   A dog with muddy paws padded across the clean kitchen floor.

3. One of my cousins is a tightrope walker in the circus.

4. Those kittens at the animal shelter need a good home.

5. By the end of the month, I have very little money in my wallet.

ADDITIONAL FACTS ABOUT VERBS

The hints that follow will further help you find the verb in a sentence.

1   Verbs do not always consist of just one word. Sometimes they consist of a main verb plus one or more **helping verbs**, such as *do, have, may, would, can, could,* or *should.* Here, for example, are some of the forms of the verb *love:*

love	could love	is loving	may have loved
loves	would love	was loving	might have loved
loved	will love	will be loving	must have loved
may love	do love	has loved	should have loved
must love	does love	have loved	could have loved
should love	did love	had loved	would have loved

2   Although words like *not, just, never, only,* and *always* may appear between the main verb and the helping verb, they are never part of the verb.

Ellen might not make the basketball team this year.

You should always count the change the cashier gives you.

That instructor can never end her class on time.

3   The verb of a sentence never comes after the word *to.*

Sal chose to live with his parents during college. (Although *live* is a verb, *to live* cannot be the verb of the sentence.)

4   A word ending in *-ing* cannot by itself be the verb of the sentence. It can be part of the verb, but it needs a helping verb before it.

The strikers were hoping for a quick settlement. (You could not correctly say, "The strikers hoping for a quick settlement.")

Practice 2

In each of the sentences below, cross out the prepositional phrases. Then underline the subject once and the verb twice.

1. Everyone at the plant is working overtime during August.

2. A list of award winners will be posted on the school's website.

3. Around midnight, a police siren began to wail in the nearby street.

4. That shirt should not have been put in the washing machine.

5. On hot days, you must always remember to provide extra water for the dog.

Note   Additional information about subjects and verbs appears on page 203.

2 More about Verbs

Seeing What You Know

For each pair, circle the letter of the sentence that you believe is correct. Then read the explanations that follow.

1. a. I brang the hot dogs to the picnic, but Jerry forgot the rolls.
   b. I brought the hot dogs to the picnic, but Jerry forgot the rolls.

2. a. Many children be afraid of thunder and lightning.
   b. Many children are afraid of thunder and lightning.

3. a. Please phone me as soon as the package arrives.
   b. Please phone me as soon as the package arrive.

4. a. Reba thought her boyfriend was faithful, but then she noticed him holding hands with another woman.
   b. Reba thought her boyfriend was faithful, but then she notices him holding hands with another woman.

Understanding the Answers

1. In the first pair, *b* is correct.
   Bring is an irregular verb; its past tense is *brought,* not *brang.*

2. In the second pair, *b* is correct.
   "Many children *be* afraid" is nonstandard English.

3. In the third pair, *a* is correct.
   Package is singular. In standard English, the verb that goes with it must end in *-s.*

4. In the fourth pair, *a* is correct.
   Since the action in the first part of the sentence is in the past *(thought her boyfriend was faithful),* the other verb in the sentence should be in the past as well *(noticed,* not *notices).*

This chapter covers three areas in which verb mistakes commonly occur: regular and irregular verbs, standard and nonstandard verbs, and shifts in verb tense.

REGULAR AND IRREGULAR VERBS

Verbs have four principal parts: the **basic form** (used to form the present tense), the **past tense**, the p~~~~~~~~~~~~ ~~~~~~~d with the helping verbs *have, has, had, is, are, was,* and *were*), and the **present participle** (~~~ ~~~~~~~~~~~~~~~~~~~~~~~~ ~~~~ plus *-ing*). All of the verb tenses come from one of the four principal parts of verbs.

Most English verbs are **regular**. That is, they form their past tense and past participle by adding *-d* or *-ed* to the basic form, like this:

Basic Form	Past Tense	Past Participle	Present Participle
ask	asked	asked	asking
drop	dropped	dropped	dropping
raise	raised	raised	raising

Irregular verbs, however, do not follow this pattern. They can have many different forms for the past and past participle. (The present participles, however, are formed in the usual way, by adding *-ing*.) Here are the four principal parts of some common irregular verbs:

Basic Form	Past Tense	Past Participle	Present Participle
become	became	become	becoming
begin	began	begun	beginning
blow	blew	blown	blowing
break	broke	broken	breaking
bring	brought	brought	bringing
catch	caught	caught	catching
choose	chose	chosen	choosing
cut	cut	cut	cutting
drink	drank	drunk	drinking
drive	drove	driven	driving
eat	ate	eaten	eating
fall	fell	fallen	falling
feel	felt	felt	feeling
find	found	found	finding
freeze	froze	frozen	freezing
get	got	got, gotten	getting
go	went	gone	going
hide	hid	hidden	hiding
keep	kept	kept	keeping
know	knew	known	knowing
lay	laid	laid	laying
leave	left	left	leaving

Basic Form	Past Tense	Past Participle	Present Participle
lend	lent	lent	lending
lie	lay	lain	lying
lose	lost	lost	losing
make	made	made	making
read	read	read	reading
ride	rode	ridden	riding
rise	rose	risen	rising
run	ran	run	running
say	said	said	saying
see	saw	seen	seeing
sell	sold	sold	selling
set	set	set	setting
shake	shook	shaken	shaking
sit	sat	sat	sitting
sleep	slept	slept	sleeping
spend	spent	spent	spending
swim	swam	swum	swimming
take	took	taken	taking
teach	taught	taught	teaching
tell	told	told	telling
think	thought	thought	thinking
throw	threw	thrown	throwing
wear	wore	worn	wearing
win	won	won	winning
write	wrote	written	writing

If you think a verb is irregular, and it is not in the list above, look it up in your dictionary. If it is irregular, the principal parts will be listed.

Practice 1

Underline the correct form of the verb in parentheses.

1. We (began, begun) to argue about which route to take to the stadium.

2. The high jumper has just (broke, broken) the world record.

3. After Gino had (ate, eaten) the salty pretzels and peanuts, he (drank, drunk) several glasses of water.

4. After the campers had (drove, driven) away, they looked back and (saw, seen) their dog running after them.

5. Before the writing course ended, students had (read, readed) fifteen essays, had (wrote, written) ten short papers, and had (took, taken) a midterm and a final exam.

STANDARD AND NONSTANDARD VERBS

Some of us are accustomed to using nonstandard English with our families and friends. Like slang, expressions such as *it ain't, we has, I be,* or *he don't* may be part of the rich language of a particular community or group.

However, nonstandard English can hold us back when used outside the home community, in both college and the working world. Standard English helps ensure that we will communicate clearly with other people, especially on the job.

The Differences between Standard and Nonstandard Verb Forms

Study the chart below, which shows both standard and nonstandard forms of the regular verb *like*. Practice using the standard forms in your speech and writing.

Nonstandard Forms		Standard Forms	
Present Tense			
I likes	we likes	I like	we like
you likes	you likes	you like	you like
he, she, it like	they likes	he, she, it likes	they like
Past Tense			
I like	we like	I liked	we liked
you like	you like	you liked	you liked
he, she, it like	they like	he, she, it liked	they liked

Notes

1 In standard English, always add *-s* or *-es* to a verb in the present tense when the subject is *he, she, it,* or any one person or thing (other than *I* or *you*).

Nonstandard: Aunt Bessie play bingo regularly at her church.
Standard: Aunt Bessie play**s** bingo regularly at her church.

2 Always add the ending *-d* or *-ed* to a regular verb to show it is past tense.

Nonstandard: Last year, Aunt Bessie play bingo 104 times.
Standard: Last year, Aunt Bessie play**ed** bingo 104 times.

Practice 2

Underline the standard form of the verb in parentheses.

1. On April Fools' Day, the principal (dress, dresses) up like a clown.

2. The fans groaned when the receiver (drop, dropped) the pass in the end zone.

3. I (look, looked) all over for my keys and finally found them in my coat pocket.

4. Most people (hate, hates) going to the dentist.

5. Though Kia moved last year, she still (manage, manages) to keep in touch.

Three Problem Verbs

Three irregular verbs that often cause special problems are *be, do,* and *have.* Non-standard English often uses forms such as *I be* (instead of *I am*), *you was* (instead of *you were*), *they has* (instead of *they have*), *he do* (instead of *he does*), and *she done* (instead of *she did*). Here are the correct present- and past-tense forms of these three verbs.

Present Tense		Past Tense	
	Be		
I am	we are	I was	we were
you are	you are	you were	you were
he, she, it is	they are	he, she, it was	they were
	Do		
I do	we do	I did	we did
you do	you do	you did	you did
he, she, it does	they do	he, she, it did	they did
	Have		
I have	we have	I had	we had
you have	you have	you had	you had
he, she, it has	they have	he, she, it had	they had

Practice 3

Underline the standard form of the verb in parentheses.

1. To my surprise, my little sister (did, done) a terrific job of cleaning the house.

2. Jamal (have, has) the best handwriting in our family.

3. You (was, were) wrong to assume that because the instructor gave you a D, he dislikes you.

4. It (doesn't, don't) make sense to sign up for a course and then not go to class.

5. Fran (were, was) halfway to the supermarket when she realized she had no money in her wallet.

SHIFTS IN VERB TENSE

In writing and in conversation, people sometimes shift from one verb tense (the form of the verb that tells us when something happened) to another. Note the tense shifts in the following passage:

> With his oversized T-shirt, the little boy looked even smaller than he was. His skinny arms extend out of the flopping sleeves that reach to his elbows. He needed a haircut; he has to brush his bangs out of his eyes to see. His eyes fail to meet those of the people passing by as he asked them, "Could you give me fifty cents?"

Although the action is in the past, the writer continuously shifts from the past tense *(boy looked . . . he was . . . He needed . . . he asked)* to the present *(arms extend . . . that reach . . . he has . . . eyes fail)*. These tense shifts will confuse a reader, who won't know when the events happened. In the above passage, the verbs should be consistently in the past tense:

> With his oversized T-shirt, the little boy looked even smaller than he was. His skinny arms extended out of the flopping sleeves that reached to his elbows. He needed a haircut; he had to brush his bangs out of his eyes to see. His eyes failed to meet those of the people passing by as he asked them, "Could you give me fifty cents?"

In your own writing, shift tenses only when the time of the action actually changes.

Practice 4

Cross out the one verb in each item that is not in the same tense as the others. Then write the correct form of that verb on the line provided.

_____   1. The mossy green log lay in the shallow water. When it began to move, I realize that it was an alligator.

_____   2. Every time my mother feels like snacking, she brushes her teeth, and the hunger disappeared.

_____   3. I came home early because I felt sick; then I discover I did not have my house key.

_____   4. The children love going to the school library because they can take out any book they wanted, even if they can't read it yet.

_____   5. After the coach yells at him, Gary thought all night about quitting the team, but then he decided to give himself one more chance.

Note   Additional information about verbs appears on pages 204–207.

Name _____ Section _____ Date _____

■ More about Verbs: Test 5

Each of the sentences in the following passage contains one of the verb problems discussed in this chapter. Underline these errors. Then, in the spaces provided, write the correct forms of the verbs.

Note   To help you master the different verb skills in this chapter, directions are given for five of the sentences.

[1]When I lived in the jungle of Costa Rica, I encounter many different types of wildlife, some of which did truly weird or scary things. [2]One morning we discovered that a monkey had ate some mangoes that we had set on the porch for our breakfast. [3]Later, an armadillo in the road jump straight up and hit the underside of our jeep. [4]Another time an armadillo stay underwater for five minutes. [5]My roommate, Julia, were surprised to find a scorpion in her bed. [6]Julia and I seen a cockroach the size of my hand above the refrigerator. [7]One night, while I was sitting at my desk, a tarantula falled onto my head. [8]I shook it off and begun screaming as it ran outside. [9]My neighbor, Diane, nearly trip over a poisonous snake on her porch. [10]Shaking with fear, Diane and I watch as the snake slithered away into the grass.

1. _____   The second verb should match the past tense form of the other verbs.

2. _____

3. _____   Use the standard English form of the regular verb *jump*.

4. _____

5. _____   Use the correct past tense form of the irregular verb *be*.

6. _____

7. _____   Use the correct past tense of the irregular verb *fall*.

8. _____

9. _____   Use the standard English form of the regular verb *trip*.

10. _____

Name _____   Section _____ Date _____

Score: (Number right) _____ × 10 = _____%

■ More about Verbs: Test 6

Each of the sentences in the following passage contains one of the verb problems discussed in this chapter. Underline these errors. Then, in the spaces provided, write the correct forms of the verbs.

¹Vincent Van Gogh were one of the greatest painters of all time. ²But during his own lifetime, people consider Van Gogh a failure, even a madman. ³Only one Van Gogh painting selled while he was alive. ⁴Van Gogh was an odd, passionate man with whom few people feeled comfortable. ⁵An illness that causes him to behave in violent, self-destructive ways made his life difficult. ⁶During one attack of this illness, he remove part of his ear with a razor. ⁷Lonely and isolated, Van Gogh throwed himself into his work. ⁸He often produce a wonderful painting in just one day. ⁹His intense, colorful paintings of sunflowers and wheat fields have became world-famous since his death, and collectors now pay millions of dollars for them. ¹⁰Sadly, Van Gogh ends his own unhappy life when he was only thirty-seven.

1. _____

2. _____

3. _____

4. _____

5. _____

6. _____

7. _____

8. _____

9. _____

10. _____

3 Subject-Verb Agreement

Seeing What You Know

Underline the verb that you think should be used in each of the following sentences. Then read the explanations below.

1. The two gray cats sitting by the trash can (belongs, belong) to a neighbor.

2. Which one of the bikes (is, are) Enrique going to buy?

3. Nobody in my family (carries, carry) a gun.

4. Chicago and Atlanta (has, have) the busiest airports in the United States.

Understanding the Answers

1. The two gray cats sitting by the trash can **belong** to a neighbor.
   The subject, *cats,* is plural, so the verb must be plural as well.

2. Which one of the bikes **is** Enrique **going** to buy?
   The subject, *Enrique,* and the verb, *is going,* are both singular.

3. Nobody in my family **carries** a gun.
   The subject, *nobody,* is a singular indefinite pronoun, so it requires a singular verb.

4. Chicago and Atlanta **have** the busiest airports in the United States.
   Chicago and Atlanta is a compound subject and requires a plural verb.

In a correctly written sentence, the subject and verb **agree** (match) **in number**. Singular subjects have singular verbs; plural subjects have plural verbs.

In a simple sentence of few words, it's not difficult to make the subject (*s*) and verb (*v*) agree:

s   *v   (plural)*   *s*   *v   (singular)*

My **parents work** at two jobs. My **grandmother takes** care of the children.

However, not all sentences are this straightforward. This chapter will present four types of situations that can pose problems in subject-verb agreement: (1) subject and verb separated by a prepositional phrase, (2) verb coming before the subject, (3) indefinite pronoun subject, and (4) compound subjects.

1 SUBJECT AND VERB SEPARATED BY A PREPOSITIONAL PHRASE

In many sentences, the subject is close to the verb, with the subject coming first. But in some sentences, the subject and verb do not appear side by side:

s   *v*

Most **stores** in the mall **are having** sales this weekend.

Who or what is the sentence about? The answer is *stores* (not *mall*). What are the stores doing? They *are having* (sales). Since the subject *(stores)* is plural, the verb *(are having)* must be plural as well.

In the sentence above, a prepositional phrase, *in the mall,* separates the subject and the verb. (A **prepositional phrase** is a group of words that begins with a preposition and ends with a noun or pronoun. *In, on, for, from, of, to,* and *by* are prepositions; a longer list of prepositions is on page 18.) Remember that the subject of the sentence is never part of a prepositional phrase. To find the subject, cross out prepositional phrases. Then make the verb agree with the subject—not with a word in the prepositional phrase.

Practice 1

Cross out the prepositional phrases in the sentences below. Then underline the subject of each sentence. Finally, double-underline the verb in parentheses that agrees with the subject.

1. The workers behind the counter (likes, like) to joke with their customers.

2. Two women on my bowling team always (scores, score) over 250.

3. The noise in the city streets sometimes (hurts, hurt) my ears.

4. A bag of nonfat potato chips (contains, contain) 440 calories.

5. The instructions for downloading software from the Internet (is, are) confusing for many people.

2 VERB COMING BEFORE THE SUBJECT

In most English sentences, the verb follows the subject. (*I saw an eagle. The knife fell to the floor. A train crashed.*) But in some sentences, the verb comes *before* the subject. These sentences often are questions, or they may begin with prepositional phrases or word groups like *there is* and *here are*. The verb must agree with the subject—even when the verb comes before the subject.

There **are** many starving **actors** in Hollywood. *(Plural verb, plural subject)*

Here **is** the computer **disk** for that project. *(Singular verb, singular subject)*

In that box **are** other **supplies**. *(Plural verb, plural subject)*

What **was** the **purpose** of that assignment? *(Singular verb, singular subject)*

If you are not sure of the subject in a sentence, find the verb and then ask "Who?" or "What?" In the first sentence above, for example, you would ask, "What are there in Hollywood?" The answer, "starving *actors,*" is the subject. For the second sentence, the question would be, "What is here?" The answer: "The computer *disk.*"

Practice 2

Cross out the prepositional phrases in the sentences below. Then underline the subject of each sentence. Finally, double-underline the verb in parentheses that agrees with the subject.

1. Where (is, are) the keys to the minivan?
2. Underneath that big rock (lives, live) hundreds of bugs.
3. There (was, were) seventeen people ahead of me in the bank line today.
4. Why (does, do) dogs always bark the loudest at 2 a.m.?
5. Inside each cardboard carton (is, are) a dozen boxes of Girl Scout cookies.

3 INDEFINITE PRONOUN SUBJECTS

The following **indefinite pronouns** always take singular verbs.

Singular Indefinite Pronouns			
each	anyone	anybody	anything
either	everyone	everybody	everything
neither	someone	somebody	something
one	no one	nobody	nothing

Note the subject-verb relationships in the following sentences with indefinite pronouns:

> **One** of those writing courses **is** still open. *(Singular subject, singular verb)*
>
> **Neither** of my parents **has** called. *(Singular subject, singular verb)*
>
> **Somebody was** reading my mail. *(Singular subject, singular verb)*
>
> **Everyone loves** to get something for nothing. *(Singular subject, singular verb)*

Practice 3

Underline the subject of each sentence. Then double-underline the verb in parentheses that agrees with the subject.

1. Everything on those shelves (is, are) on sale at 50 percent off.

2. Neither of the lights in the basement (works, work).

3. No one in my family (is, are) right-handed.

4. Each of those kittens (deserves, deserve) a good home.

5. Everybody in my apartment building (knows, know) when someone is having a party.

4 COMPOUND SUBJECTS

A **compound subject**—usually two or more subjects joined by *and*—requires a plural verb.

> Rent and car insurance **were** my biggest expenses each month.
>
> There **are** canoes and sailboats for rent.
>
> **Do** the TV and DVD player **provide** stereo sound?

Practice 4

Underline the compound subject of each sentence. Then double-underline the verb in parentheses that agrees with the compound subject.

1. Our cats and dog (stays, stay) at a neighbor's house when we go on vacation.

2. (Is, Are) all the CDs and DVDs in the store included in the sale?

3. Staples and Scotch tape (holds, hold) all the old record album covers together.

4. The scratches and dents on our new car (was, were) definitely our son's fault.

5. My accounting course and my statistics course (requires, require) long written reports.

Note   Additional information about subject-verb agreement appears on pages 208–209.

4 Sentence Types

Seeing What You Know

A. In each blank, add a word that fits the sentence.

1. The noisy _____ woke the baby.

2. The forest ranger _____ at the campers.

B. In each sentence that follows, insert *and, but,* or *so*. Use each word once.

3. My pencil is broken, _____ my pen is out of ink.

4. The pool is closed, _____ we can't go swimming.

5. I have an envelope, _____ I can't find a stamp.

C. In each sentence that follows, insert *after, although,* or *because*. Use each word once.

6. We called an exterminator _____ we have termites.

7. _____ their big fight, Jessica sent her boyfriend flowers.

8. _____ my closet is full of clothes, I have nothing to wear.

Understanding the Answers

A. Sentence 1 could be completed with a subject such as *party;* the verb is *woke*. Sentence 2 could be completed with a verb such as *waved;* the subject is *ranger.*

Some sentences in English are **simple**, made up of one subject-verb combination expressing a complete thought. Sentences 1 and 2 are examples of simple sentences.

B. You should have inserted *and* in sentence 3, *so* in 4, and *but* in 5.

Other sentences are **compound**, made up of two or more complete thoughts connected by a joining word such as *and, so,* or *but*. Sentences 3–5 are all compound sentences.

C. You should have inserted *because* in sentence 6, *after* in 7, and *although* in 8.

Yet other sentences are **complex**, made up of one complete thought and at least one dependent thought. Dependent thoughts begin with a dependent word such as *because, although,* or *after*. Sentences 6–8 are all complex sentences.

hree most basic kinds of sentences in English are simple, compound, and
'ex sentences. This chapter explains and provides practice in all three sen-
ten   es. It also discusses two types of words you can use to combine ideas
into   tence: (1) joining words (for compound sentences) and (2) dependent
wor s (t   es).

THE SIMPLE SENTENCE

A s **nple sentence** has only one subject-verb combination and expresses a
ple thought.

An owl hooted.

The winning contestant could have chosen money or a car.

A   nple sentence may have more than one subject:

Lemons and limes taste sharp and tangy.

(In this sentence, *lemons* and *limes* are the subjects.)

A   mple sentence may have more than one verb:

The puppies nipped and nuzzled one another playfully.

(In this sentence, *nipped* and *nuzzled* are the verbs.)

A   mple sentence may even have   jects and verbs:

Every New Year'   y parents, aunts, and uncles eat, dance, and welcome
the new year   ther.

(There are   ubjects in this sentence: *parents, aunts,* and *uncles.* There
are also thre   : *eat, dance,* and *welcome.*)

Practice 1

Complete the simple   ences below by filling in one or more subjects, one or
m   e verbs, or both.

The _____ _____ is unusually crowded today.

A thoughtless driv _____ an empty soda can onto the
highway.

_____ ____ and _____ make a delicious
sandwich combinat.

Mike and _____ _____ often _____ together
in the park.

_____ ____ and _____ looked at old family

photographs and the _____ dinner on the porch.

THE COMPOUND SENTENCE

A **compound sentence** is made up of two or more complete thoughts. For instance, look at the following simple sentences:

> Supper is ready.

> The guests have not arrived.

These two simple sentences can be combined to form one compound sentence:

> Supper is ready, **but** the guests have not arrived.

The process of joining two ideas of equal importance is known as **coordination**. Put a comma plus a joining word (also known as a **coordinating conjunction**), such as *and, but,* or *so,* between the two complete thoughts. Other joining words— *or, for, nor,* and *yet*—appear on pages 73 and 212–213.

> The cover is torn off this book, **and** the last few pages are missing. (**And** means *in addition:* The cover is torn off this book; *in addition,* the last few pages are missing.)

> The kittens are darling, **but** we can't have another pet. (**But** means *however:* The kittens are darling; *however,* we can't have another pet.)

> Kendra has to get up early tomorrow, **so** she isn't going to the party tonight. (**So** means *as a result:* Kendra has to get up early tomorrow; *as a result,* she isn't going to the party tonight.)

Practice 2

Use a comma and a suitable joining word to combine each pair of simple sentences into a compound sentence. Use each of the following joining words **once.**

and	**but**	**so**

1. Rodrigo is usually cheerful.
   He seems quiet and troubled today.

   _____

   _____

2. All my clothes were dirty this morning.
   I'm wearing my husband's shirt.

   _____

   _____

3. Virginia has learned karate.
   She carries a can of self-defense spray.

   _____

   _____

THE COMPLEX SENTENCE

As you have learned, a compound sentence is made up of two or more complete thoughts. Each thought could stand alone as an independent statement. A **complex sentence**, on the other hand, includes one independent statement and at least one dependent statement, which *cannot* stand alone. Look at the following example:

If it thunders, our dog hides under the bed.

The second statement in this sentence is **independent**. It can stand alone as a simple sentence: *Our dog hides under the bed.* The first statement, however, cannot stand alone. It is **dependent**—it depends on the rest of the sentence to finish the thought *If it thunders.* Dependent statements begin with dependent words (also known as subordinating conjunctions), such as *after, although, as, because, when,* and *while.* (A full list is on page 60.) A dependent statement also includes a subject and a verb. (The subject of the dependent statement above is *it;* the verb is *thunders.*)

Punctuation note   Put a comma at the end of a dependent statement that begins a sentence, as in the example above.

Practice 3

Combine each pair of simple sentences into a complex sentence. To change a simple sentence into a dependent statement, add a dependent word to it, as shown in the example. Choose a suitable dependent word from the following:

after   **although**   **as**

Use each word **once**. Put a comma after a dependent statement that starts a sentence.

Example   We ate the pork chops with our hands.
           We were out of clean silverware.

We ate the pork chops with our hands because we were out of clean silverware.

1. The familiar "Wedding March" played.
   The bride and her father walked down the aisle.

   _____

   _____

2. Jeff broke out in red blotches.
   He walked through a bank of poison ivy.

   _____

   _____

3. Mei Lin scrubbed for an hour.
   She could not get the crayon marks off the wall.

   _____

   _____

5 Fragments

Seeing What You Know

Underline the statement in each item that you think is *not* a complete sentence. Then read the explanations below.

1. After the shopping mall opened. Several local stores went out of business.

2. The nursing student poked my arm four times. Trying to take a blood sample. I was beginning to feel like a pincushion.

3. Some young people are learning old-fashioned dances. Such as the waltz, polka, and Lindy.

4. The manager always wears a suit and tie to the office. Then takes off his jacket and tie by ten o'clock.

Understanding the Answers

1. *After the shopping mall opened* is not a complete sentence.
   The writer does not follow through and complete the thought by telling us what happened after the shopping mall opened. Correct the fragment by adding it to the sentence that follows it.

2. *Trying to take a blood sample* is not a complete sentence.
   The word group lacks both a subject and a verb, and it does not express a complete thought. Correct the fragment by adding it to the sentence that precedes it.

3. *Such as the waltz, polka, and Lindy* is not a complete sentence.
   Again, the word group lacks a subject and a verb, and it does not express a complete thought. Correct the fragment by adding it to the sentence that precedes it.

4. *Then takes off his jacket and tie by ten o'clock* is not a complete sentence.
   The word group lacks a subject. Correct the fragment by adding the subject *he*.

To be a complete sentence, a group of words must contain a subject and a verb. It must also express a complete thought—in other words, it must make sense by itself. A **fragment** is *less than a sentence* because it lacks a subject, lacks a verb, or does not express a complete thought.

This chapter describes the most common types of fragments: dependent-word fragments, *-ing* and *to* fragments, added-detail fragments, and missing-subject fragments.

DEPENDENT-WORD FRAGMENTS

Although dependent-word fragments contain a subject and a verb, they do not express a complete thought. To complete the thought, they depend on another statement, usually one that comes after the fragment. For instance, below is a word group that starts with the dependent word *because.* The incomplete thought it expresses is completed in the statement that follows it.

Because there was a mosquito in the room. I could not fall asleep.

The dependent-word group is a fragment because it does not express a complete thought. It leaves the reader expecting something more. The writer must follow through *in the same sentence* and tell what happened because there was a mosquito in the room. In the sentence below, the writer has corrected the fragment by completing the thought in one sentence:

Because there was a mosquito in the room, I could not fall asleep.

Here is a list of some common dependent words:

Dependent Words				
after	even if	since	until	wherever
although	even though	so that	what	whether
as	how	that	when	which
because	if	though	whenever	while
before	in order that	unless	where	who

Whenever you begin a statement with a dependent word, make sure that you complete your thought. Look at the following examples:

Although we had eaten a full meal. We still ordered dessert. The rum cake was irresistible.

Some people are victims of migraine headaches. That force them to lie motionless in bed for many hours. Medications do not offer much relief.

The word groups that begin with the dependent words *although* and *that* are fragments. Neither word group expresses a complete thought. The reader wants to know *what happened* although a full meal had been eaten and *what* forces people to lie motionless in bed for many hours.

A common way to correct a dependent-word fragment is to connect it to the sentence that comes before or after it. For example,

Although we had eaten a full **meal, we** still ordered dessert. The rum cake was irresistible.

Some people are victims of migraine **headaches that** force them to lie motionless in bed for many hours. Medications do not offer much relief.

Punctuation note   Put a comma at the end of a dependent-word group that starts a sentence. (See the first example above.)

Practice 1

Underline the dependent-word fragment in each of the following. Then correct it on the lines provided.

1. When the hometown baseball team won the World Series. Two million people showed up at the victory parade.

   _____

   _____

2. Because smoke detectors are so important to a family's safety. Their batteries should be checked often.

   _____

   _____

3. After the children washed the family car. They had a water fight with the wet sponges.

   _____

   _____

4. Please hang up the damp towel. That you just threw on the floor.

   _____

   _____

-*ING* AND *TO* FRAGMENTS

When -*ing* or *to* appears at or near the beginning of a word group, a fragment may result. Consider this example:

Cliff sat by the telephone for hours. Hoping that Lisa would call.

The first statement is a complete sentence. However, the second word group is not a complete thought, so it cannot stand on its own as a sentence.

Consider the following example as well:

To balance their checkbooks without making mistakes. Many people use pocket calculators.

The second statement is a complete sentence. But the first word group lacks a subject and verb *and* fails to express a complete thought.

There are two ways to correct *-ing* and *to* fragments:

a　Connect an *-ing* or a *to* fragment to the sentence it explains.

Cliff sat by the telephone for **hours, hoping** that Lisa would call.

To balance their checkbooks without making **mistakes, many** people use pocket calculators.

b　Create a complete sentence by adding a subject and a verb to the fragment. To do so, revise the material as necessary.

Cliff sat by the telephone for hours. **He hoped** that Lisa would call.

Many people use pocket calculators. **They want** to balance their checkbooks without making mistakes.

Practice 2

Underline the *-ing* or *to* fragment in each of the following. Then correct it on the lines provided, using one of the two methods given above.

1. Police officers stood near the corner. Directing people around the accident.

   _____

   _____

2. The magician ran a sword through the box. To prove no one was hiding inside.

   _____

   _____

3. Sitting quietly on the couch. The dog didn't look as if he'd eaten my sandwich.

   _____

   _____

4. The restaurant has introduced a new vegetarian menu. To attract diners who prefer not to eat meat.

   _____

   _____

ADDED-DETAIL FRAGMENTS

Another common kind of fragment often begins with one of the following words: *like, including, especially, also, for example, for instance, except, without,* or *such as.*

Almost everyone loves ice cream. Especially vanilla.

Many college students experience a great deal of stress. For instance, about money, grades, and personal relationships.

In the above examples, the second word group lacks both a subject and a verb. There are two ways to correct an added-detail fragment:

a Simply add the fragment to the sentence it explains. In most cases, use a comma to set off the fragment from the rest of the sentence.

Almost everyone loves ice **cream, especially** vanilla.

b Create a new sentence by adding a subject and verb to the fragment.

Many college students experience a great deal of stress. For instance, **they worry** about money, grades, and personal relationships.

Practice 3

Underline the added-detail fragment in each of the following. Then correct it on the lines provided, using one of the two methods given above.

1. Television censors watch out for material that viewers might find offensive. Such as sexual or racial jokes.

   _____

   _____

2. The children's toys were everywhere. Except in the toy chest.

   _____

   _____

3. All applicants at that company must take a skills assessment test. Also a personality profile test.

   _____

   _____

4. The film class saw every Dustin Hoffman film. Including his first one, *The Graduate.*

   _____

   _____

MISSING-SUBJECT FRAGMENTS

Some word groups are fragments because, while they do have a verb, they lack a subject. Here are examples:

> The telephone caller kept asking questions. But did not identify herself.
>
> The children dug a large hole in the grass. And then tried to fill it with water.

There are two ways to correct a missing-subject fragment:

a   Connect the missing-subject fragment to the sentence it follows.

> The telephone caller kept asking **questions but** did not identify herself.
>
> The children dug a large hole in the **grass and** then tried to fill it with water.

b   Create a new sentence by adding a subject to the fragment. Normally, you will add a pronoun standing for the subject of the previous sentence.

> The telephone caller kept asking questions. **She** did not identify herself.
>
> The children dug a large hole in the grass. Then **they** tried to fill it with water.

Practice 4

Underline the missing-subject fragment in each of the following items. Then correct it on the lines below, using one of the two methods given above.

1. Our instructor seems strict. But is actually friendly and helpful.

   _____

   _____

2. A mouse's face popped out of a hole near the sink. Then disappeared quickly.

   _____

   _____

3. The nurse brought the patient an extra pillow and a glass of water. But forgot his pain medication.

   _____

   _____

4. The pot of coffee sat on the burner for hours. And became too strong and bitter to drink.

   _____

   _____

Note   Not all word groups beginning with *and, but, so,* or another joining word are fragments. A sentence beginning with a joining word is grammatically complete—and correct—if both a subject and a verb follow the joining word.

6 Run-Ons and Comma Splices

Seeing What You Know

Read the following pairs of items and, for each pair, check the item that is punctuated correctly. Then read the explanations below.

1. ___ a. Our math professor has the flu, half the class is sick as well.

   ___ b. Our math professor has the flu, and half the class is sick as well.

2. ___ a. Sue seldom got to play in an actual game. She was tempted to quit the team.

   ___ b. Sue seldom got to play in an actual game she was tempted to quit the team.

3. ___ a. My father had no brothers or sisters, he never learned to share.

   ___ b. Because my father had no brothers or sisters, he never learned to share.

Understanding the Answers

1. Item *b* is punctuated correctly.

   Item *a* is a comma splice. It is made up of two complete statements that are incorrectly connected by only a comma. In item *b*, the two statements are correctly connected—by a comma and a joining word, *and*.

2. Item *a* is punctuated correctly.

   Item *b* is a run-on sentence. It is made up of two complete statements: (1) *Sue seldom got to play in an actual game.* (2) *She was tempted to quit the team.* In item *a,* each of these two complete thoughts is stated in a separate sentence.

3. Item *b* is punctuated correctly.

   Item *a* is a comma splice. It is made up of two complete statements: (1) *My father had no brothers or sisters.* (2) *He never learned to share.* In item *b,* the first statement is subordinated to the second statement with the addition of the dependent word *because.*

Run-on sentences and **comma splices** are the opposite of fragments. They are *more than a sentence* because they combine two complete thoughts without putting appropriate words or punctuation between them. This chapter will show you how to recognize and correct run-ons and comma splices.

RUN-ONS

When there is *no punctuation at all* separating two complete statements, the result is a **run-on**, also called a **fused sentence**. The two statements are simply fused, or run together, into one sentence.

Complete statement 1: Test anxiety is a very real condition.

Complete statement 2: Some symptoms are stomach cramps and headaches.

Run-on: Test anxiety is a very real condition some symptoms are stomach cramps and headaches.

Complete statement 1: Computer skills are useful in college.

Complete statement 2: They will help you in the job market as well.

Run-on: Computer skills are useful in college they will help you in the job market as well.

A good way to prevent run-ons is to read your work aloud. You will naturally tend to pause between complete thoughts. Also look within the sentence for words like *I, you, he, she, it, we, they, there, this, that, now, then,* and *next.* Such words often signal the beginning of a second complete thought. (See page 211 for other words that can lead to run-ons.)

Correcting Run-Ons

Here are three methods of correcting a run-on:

1 Divide the run-on into two sentences.

Run-on: Test anxiety is a very real condition some symptoms are stomach cramps and headaches.

Corrected: Test anxiety is a very real condition. **S**ome symptoms are stomach cramps and headaches.

2 Put a comma plus a joining word (such as *and, but,* or *so*) between the two complete statements.

Run-on: Computer skills are useful in college they will help you in the job market as well.

Corrected: Computer skills are useful in college, **and** they will help you in the job market as well.

Run-on: I'd love to go out to eat tonight I'm short of money right now.

Corrected: I'd love to go out to eat tonight, **but** I'm short of money right now.

Run-on: Carmen has a broken foot she won't do any hiking this fall.

Corrected: Carmen has a broken foot, **so** she won't do any hiking this fall.

Note 1   Be sure to use a logical joining word. In the first example, *and* is appropriate because it means *in addition.* (Computer skills are useful in college; *in addition,* they will help you in the job market as well.) In the second example, *but* is appropriate because it means *however.* (I'd love to go out to eat tonight; *however,* I'm short of money right now.) In the third example, *so* means *as a result.* (Carmen has a broken foot; *as a result,* she won't do any hiking this fall.)

Note 2   The comma always goes *before* the joining word—not after it.

Note 3   Other joining words are *for* (which means *because*), *or, nor,* and *yet* (which means *however*). (For information on when to use these words, see pages 212–213.)

3   Use subordination to make one of the complete thoughts dependent on the other one.

To subordinate a complete thought, change it from a statement that can stand alone as a sentence to one that cannot stand by itself. To do so, begin the thought with an appropriate dependent word, such as *because, when, if, before, since, until, unless, while, as, although,* and *after.* (Additional dependent words appear on page 60.)

Run-on: Carmen has a broken foot she won't do any hiking this fall.

Corrected: **Because** Carmen has a broken foot, she won't do any hiking this fall.

Important punctuation note   Be sure to put a comma at the end of a dependent-word group that begins a sentence.

Practice 1

Draw a slash (/) between the two complete thoughts in each of the fused sentences that follow. Then correct each fused sentence, using one of the methods described above. Use a different method for each sentence.

1. It's easy to begin smoking it's much harder to quit.

   _____

   _____

2. Some people at the office have gotten raises the other workers are jealous.

   _____

   _____

3. The patient's blood pressure was low his temperature was low as well.

   _____

   _____

COMMA SPLICES

When a comma alone separates two complete thoughts, the result is called a **comma splice**. A comma alone is not enough to mark the break between complete statements. Something stronger is needed.

> *Complete statement 1:* Kevin was always nervous about tests.
>
> *Complete statement 2:* His grades were usually the highest in the class.
>
> *Comma splice:*   Kevin was always nervous about tests, his grades were usually the highest in the class.

Correcting Comma Splices

A comma splice can be corrected by using one of the same three methods suggested for correcting a run-on:

1   Divide the comma splice into two sentences: Kevin was always nervous about tests. **H**is grades were usually the highest in the class.

2   Connect the two complete thoughts by placing a joining word (such as *and, but,* or *so*) after the comma: Kevin was always nervous about tests**, but** his grades were usually the highest in the class.

3   Use subordination (add a dependent word to one of the complete thoughts): Kevin was always nervous about tests **although** his grades were usually the highest in the class.

Practice 2

Correct each of the comma splices that follow, using one of the methods described above. Use a different method for each sentence.

1. Hakim was talking on the phone, he was switching TV channels with his remote control at the same time.

    _____

    _____

2. I chose the shortest checkout line at the supermarket, then the one customer in front of me pulled out dozens of coupons.

    _____

    _____

3. The electricity at Jasmin's house went out, she had to write her paper by candlelight.

    _____

    _____

Note   Additional information about run-ons and comma splices appears on pages 210–211.

7 Pronouns

Seeing What You Know

Cross out the pronoun mistake in each of the following sentences, and write the corrections above the mistakes. Then read the explanations below.

1. Each of my sons required two chances to pass their driver's test.

2. If there are stains on any hotel towels, they should be removed immediately.

3. I don't shop at that supermarket because they are so slow at the check-out counters.

4. People go to the local diner because you can get low-priced meals there all day.

Understanding the Answers

1. Each of my sons required two chances to pass **his** driver's test.
   Each is singular. It needs a singular pronoun, *his,* to refer to it.

2. If there are stains on any hotel towels, **the towels** should be removed immediately.
   Which does the writer want us to remove—the stains or the towels? The pronoun *they* could refer to either one. Replacing *they* with *the towels* makes the meaning of the sentence clear.

3. I don't shop at that supermarket because **the clerks** are so slow at the checkout counters.
   Who are *they*? The word *they* doesn't refer to anything specific. The sentence should be clarified by replacing *they* with what it is meant to represent.

4. People go to the local diner because **they** can get low-priced meals there all day.
   People requires a third-person pronoun, *they.* Sentences that begin in the third person should not suddenly shift their point of view to the second person, *you.*

Pronouns are words that stand for nouns (names of persons, places, or things). Personal pronouns are *I, me, my, mine, you, your, yours, he, him, his, she, her, hers, it, its, we, us, our, ours, they, them, their,* and *theirs.*

Freddy is a wrestler. **He** weighs 270 pounds. (*He* stands for *Freddy.*)

Rita always writes **her** letters in purple ink. (*Her* stands for *Rita's.*)

"If **my** kids talk back, **I** let **them** know **they** are asking for trouble," Jeff said. (*My* stands for *Jeff's; I* stands for *Jeff. Them* and *they* stand for *kids.*)

This chapter shows you how to avoid the three most frequent kinds of pronoun mistakes: in pronoun agreement, in pronoun reference, and in pronoun point of view. (Additional information about pronouns appears on pages 4–5 and 189–193.)

PRONOUN AGREEMENT

A pronoun must agree in number with the word it refers to (sometimes called the pronoun's **antecedent**). Singular words require singular pronouns; plural words require plural pronouns.

The book Henry lent me is missing **its** cover. (*Its,* a singular pronoun, refers to *book,* a singular noun.)

If your cousins don't get here soon, **they** will miss the movie. (*They,* a plural pronoun, refers to *cousins,* a plural noun.)

The indefinite pronouns listed below are always singular. (See also page 41.)

Singular Indefinite Pronouns			
each	anyone	anybody	anything
either	everyone	everybody	everything
neither	someone	somebody	something
one	no one	nobody	nothing

Each of the wild horses raced for **its** freedom.

Neither of my sisters ever feels like cleaning **her** room.

No one in the class wanted to read **his** (or **her**) paper out loud.

Note   In the last example, choose a pronoun that fits the situation. If all the members of the class are male, use *his.* If they all are female, use *her.* If the class includes both men and women, use *his or her:*

No one in the class wanted to read **his or her** paper out loud.

Or avoid the extra words by rewriting the sentence in the plural:

No **students** in the class wanted to read **their papers** out loud.

Practice 1

Underline the correct word or words in the parentheses in the sentences below.

1. Each of the actresses who auditioned believes (she / they) should be chosen for the starring role.

2. Many high schools now require (its / their) students to take a computer course.

3. If anybody here has a cell phone, (they / he or she) should turn it off now so that it doesn't ring during the performance.

4. Either exercise is fine, but (it / they) must be done regularly to do any good.

5. Somebody in the men's locker room hid Paco's clothes, and Paco would love to get back at (him / them).

PRONOUN REFERENCE

A pronoun must also refer *clearly* to the word it stands for. If the meaning of a pronoun is uncertain, the sentence will be confusing. For example,

Gloria told Renée that she had gotten an A on her paper. (Who got the A—Gloria or Renée? The words *she* and *her* could refer to either one.)

I wanted a ham and cheese sandwich, but they were all out of cheese. (Who was all out of cheese? The word *they* has no one to refer to.)

There were no questions after the lecture, which was regrettable. (What was regrettable—the lecture or the lack of questions? Be careful how you use the pronouns *which* and *this*. They must clearly refer to *one* thing or situation.)

Both of Ben's parents are accountants, but this doesn't interest Ben. (What doesn't interest Ben? The pronoun *this* doesn't refer to anything in the sentence.)

To avoid mistakes like these, simply write what you mean by the pronoun.

Gloria told Renee, "**You** got an A on **your** paper."

Or: Gloria told Renee, "**I** got an A on **my** paper."

I wanted a ham and cheese sandwich, but **the deli** was all out of cheese.

There were no questions after the lecture. **Not having questions** was regrettable.

Both of Ben's parents are accountants, but **accounting** doesn't interest Ben.

Practice 2

Underline the correct word or words in the parentheses in the sentences below.

1. When Roy told his father about the surprise party, (he / his father) grinned.

2. Students complain that (they / the maintenance people) keep the library too hot.

3. While Eric was adding sugar to his coffee, he spilled (it / the sugar) all over the table.

4. Someone offered to show me a copy of next week's history test, but I said that I didn't believe in (this / cheating).

5. Many older people shop at the mall because (they / the stores) give a 15 percent discount to senior citizens.

PRONOUN POINT OF VIEW

Pronouns are either **first person** (referring to the speaker), **second person** (referring to the one spoken to), or **third person** (referring to everyone else):

	First person	Second person	Third person
Singular	I, me, my, mine	you, your, yours	he, him, his; she, her, hers; it, its
Plural	we, us, our, ours	you, your, yours	they, them, their, theirs

When you write, your pronoun point of view must stay the same. Do not shift unnecessarily from one point of view to another, as in the following sentences:

What **I** like best about vacations is that **you** don't have to set an alarm.

The **workers** here have to take a break at 10:30 whether **we** want to or not.

Instead, write the entire sentence in the same person:

What **I** like best about vacations is that **I** don't have to set an alarm.

The **workers** here have to take a break at 10:30 whether **they** want to or not.

Practice 3

Underline the correct pronoun in the parentheses in the sentences below.

1. I know spring is really here when (I / you) see neighborhood kids playing softball.

2. My father says he prefers to drive at night because then the sun won't get in (his / your) eyes.

3. First-year students at this school are required to take a math course. (You / They) must also take a computer course.

4. Although Sharon and I were good friends, (we / you) could tell that we would not be good roommates.

5. If you want to advance in this company, (we / you) must be willing to work overtime and to move to a new location every couple of years.

Note   Additional information about pronouns appears on pages 4–5 and 189–193.

Name _____ Section _____ Date _____

Score: (Number right) _____ × 10 = _____%

■ Pronouns: Test 1

Underline the correct word or words in the parentheses in the sentences below.

Note   To help you recognize and correct pronoun mistakes, explanations are given for half of the items.

1. Neither of the sisters likes to do (her / their) chores.

    Neither, an indefinite pronoun, is singular. The second pronoun must agree with it in number.

2. If anyone doesn't want (his or her / their) dessert, I'll eat it.

3. My mother told my girlfriend (she looked marvelous. / , "You look marvelous.")

    The pronoun *she* could refer to either *my mother* or *my girlfriend.*

4. Mrs. Owen told her daughter (that she couldn't babysit Friday night. / , "I can't babysit Friday night.")

5. When you drive from New York to South Carolina, (you / one) should plan to stay overnight at a motel on the way.

    The sentence begins in the second person (*you*). Do not shift the pronoun point of view.

6. We don't want the local clinic to close because then (you / we) would have to drive all the way to the city for medical treatment.

7. Both travel agents thought that (she / they) had won the free trip to Hawaii.

    Agents is plural. The second pronoun must agree in number.

8. For Halloween, Dave and Scott both dressed up in (his / their) sisters' cheer-leading uniforms.

9. When Lian learned that her new sister-in-law was a Navy pilot, she became interested in (it / a Navy career) too.

    For the sentence to be clear, the writer must state what Lian is interested in.

10. Many people enjoy hiking and camping, but I'm not interested in (them / those activities).

Name _____   _____ Section _____ Date _____

Score: (Number right) _____ × 12.5 = _____%

■ Pronouns: st 2

Underline t'   pronoun mistake in each of the sentences that follow. Then correct the mistak   y rewriting the sentence in the space provided.

1. Mari   old the manager that he needed to hire more help.

   _____

   _____

2. '   h of the sisters is a successful artist in their own field.

   _____

   _____

   I won't go to the concert tonight because there's no way you could get a ticket.

   _____

   _____

4. Maria enjoys reading to her little girl even though she sometimes gets sleepy during the stories.

   _____

   _____

5. Any basketball player who fails a course will lose their scholarship.

   _____

   _____

6. Every time Barb paints her nails, I have to leave the room because the smell of it makes me sick.

   _____

   _____

7. Many people love trying foreign restaurants where you can experience a whole new way of cooking.

   _____

   _____

8. When I was stopped for speeding, he said I'd been going fifteen miles over the limit.

   _____

   _____

Name _____ Section _____ Date _____

Score: (Number right) _____ × 10 = _____%

■ Pronouns: Test 3

Each of the following passages contains **two** pronoun mistakes. Find and underline these two mistakes. Then write the corrections in the spaces provided.

Note   To help you recognize and correct pronoun mistakes, explanations are given for the first error in each passage.

1. My friend wanted to lose weight, but she was convinced you would have to starve to do so. Then she joined an online dieting site, where they encourage each other. She ended up losing twenty pounds.

   a. _____   *You* is a shift in pronoun point
   b. _____   of view.

2. I wear disposable contact lenses instead of glasses because I find them more comfortable. However, it's easy for you to forget to change the lenses every week.

   a. _____   *Them* could refer to either the lenses
   b. _____   or the glasses.

3. In the department store, women often block the aisles and spray perfume samples on the shoppers. This annoys many people, so you have to avoid that part of the store.

   a. _____   *This* could refer to either blocking
   b. _____   the aisles or spraying the perfume.

4. Although every person has the right to their own opinion, heckling a speaker is not the way to express a view. Instead, one should picket a speech or write a letter to their local newspaper.

   a. _____   *Every person* is singular and
   b. _____   requires a singular pronoun.

5. Bob told Luis that he needed a new car. Bob went on to say, "I still like my old Corvette, but the car spends more time in the garage than on the road." Luis agreed that anybody who had to pay for so many repairs to their car should buy a new one.

   a. _____   *He* could refer to either Bob
   b. _____   or Luis.

Name _____ Section _____ Date _____

Score: (Number right) _____ × 10 = _____ %

■ Pronouns: Test 4

Each of the following passages contains **two** pronoun mistakes. Find and underline these two mistakes. Then write the corrections in the spaces provided.

1. The thing that customers like about shopping at McRay's Hardware is that you get a great deal of assistance from the clerks there. He must spend a lot of time training people after he hires them.

   a. _____

   b. _____

2. Everyone in my family was late to their job on Tuesday. A storm had knocked down power lines during the night. The utility plant got all of their workers to restore power, but most people's alarm clocks fell behind by two hours during the outage.

   a. _____

   b. _____

3. Denise was so tired last night that she went to bed without washing her face. When she woke up this morning, most of her makeup had worn off her face, and it was all over the pillow. "This is disgusting," she thought.

   a. _____

   b. _____

4. A well-known columnist advises us not to respond to e-mail messages from strangers. Somebody who tries to start a relationship by e-mail could be lying about their age, marital status, or even gender. Or the writer could be tempting us to go to a Web site where your password or credit card number will be stolen.

   a. _____

   b. _____

5. As we watched, two movers carried the piano out to their double-parked van, then left it in the middle of the street while they went for coffee. Fifteen minutes later, the movers had still not come back, and you could see cars backed up for several blocks.

   a. _____

   b. _____

Name _____   Section _____   Date _____

Score: (Number right) _____ × 10 = _____%

■ Pronouns: Test 5

Each sentence in the following passage contains one pronoun mistake. Find and underline these ten mistakes. Then write the corrections on the lines below.

Note   To help you recognize and correct pronoun mistakes, explanations are given for five of the errors.

¹When Aunt Rose and Uncle Morris finally arrived, we all jumped up from the dinner table and rushed to the door, shouting their greetings. ²"I'm sorry we're late," said Morris, "but Rose insists on driving forty-five miles an hour, no matter how late you are." ³"But don't forget we were late in coming home from shopping and also in leaving the house, and it's your fault," Rose teased. ⁴"The worst thing for me about living with Morris is you always have to wait for him to finish selecting his wardrobe, trimming his beard, and combing his hair just right." ⁵Then everyone sat back down to eat, and Rose told her sister Nancy that her red dress fit better than ever. ⁶Both Morris and his brother-in-law ate more than his share of the roast beef. ⁷The dinner was interrupted when Mr. Nichols came to the door and said, "Sorry to bother you, folks, but someone parked their car partly in front of my driveway. ⁸This could lead to a scratched and dented car—unless the car gets moved." ⁹Rose had stepped out of the room for a minute, and Morris responded, "I told Rose that nobody would be able to get their car around ours if she parked there—I'll go park the car somewhere else." ¹⁰When Uncle Morris went to move the car, the rest of us immediately sprang into action—quickly clearing the table, hanging up streamers, bringing out their presents, and opening the back door to let in the other guests for Morris's surprise birthday party.

1. _____
   We is a first-person pronoun. *Their* is a shift to the third-person point of view.

2. _____

3. _____
   It does not refer to anything in the sentence.

4. _____

5. _____
   The pronoun *her* could refer to either Rose or Nancy.

6. _____

7. _____
   Someone is an indefinite pronoun. Indefinite pronouns are singular and need another singular pronoun to keep the point of view consistent.

8. _____

9. _____
   Nobody is an indefinite pronoun, so it is singular. *Their* is plural.

10. _____

Name _____ Section _____ Date _____

Score: (Number right) _____ × 10 = _____ %

■ Pronouns: Test 6

Each sentence in the following passage contains one pronoun mistake. Find and underline these ten mistakes. Then write the corrections on the lines below.

[1]Anyone who is involved in an auto accident may have to decide whether to drive their car afterward or have it towed to a repair shop. [2]Drivers usually consider expense and convenience, but you should also know about another important factor: safety. [3]Obviously, some cars are so badly wrecked in an accident that driving it is impossible. [4]After a less serious accident, many drivers reluctantly pay high repair bills for their cars, saying they must not have been very well made in the first place if a little accident could cause all this harm. [5]However, some people with damaged cars say they would rather keep driving the car as it is. [6]If people knew more about a car's frame, they might look at this differently. [7]Many people do not realize that his or her car's frame is designed to protect them by absorbing the impact of a collision. [8]The frame may crumple, sustaining damage that is far from the point of impact; some of it may not even be visible to the naked eye. [9]Everyone should keep in mind that their car frame is designed to absorb the impact of only *one* crash. [10]A bent car frame cannot properly protect against another collision, and they risk serious injury by riding in a damaged car.

    1. _____

    2. _____

    3. _____

    4. _____

    5. _____

    6. _____

    7. _____

    8. _____

    9. _____

  10. _____

8 Comma

Seeing What You Know

Insert commas where needed in the following sentences. Then read the explanations below.

1. The restaurant dessert tray featured carrot cake coconut cream pie and something called death-by-chocolate.

2. Because I was three hours short of graduation requirements I had to take a course during the summer.

3. The weather according to last night's forecast will improve by Saturday.

4. Students hurried to the campus store to buy their fall textbooks but several of the books were already out of stock.

5. My sister asked "Are you going to be on the phone much longer?"

Understanding the Answers

1. The restaurant dessert tray featured carrot cake, coconut cream pie, and something called death-by-chocolate.
   Commas are needed to separate the items in a series.

2. Because I was three hours short of graduation requirements, I had to take a course during the summer.
   The comma separates the introductory words from the rest of the sentence.

3. The weather, according to last night's forecast, will improve by Saturday.
   The words *according to last night's forecast* interrupt the flow of the rest of the sentence, so they are set off by commas.

4. Students hurried to the campus store to buy their fall textbooks, but several of the books were already out of stock.
   The comma separates two complete thoughts connected by the joining word *but*.

5. My sister asked, "Are you going to be on the phone much longer?"
   The comma separates a direct quotation from the rest of the sentence.

This chapter explains five main uses of the comma.

1 BETWEEN ITEMS IN A SERIES

Commas are used to separate three or more items in a series.

> Bears, chipmunks, raccoons, and groundhogs all hibernate during the winter.
>
> Felipe groaned when he learned that his exams in biology, economics, and sociology were scheduled for the same day.
>
> The mechanic started the engine, fiddled with the fan belt, and announced that the problem was solved.

But Do not use a comma when the series contains only two items.
> The mechanic started the engine and fiddled with the fan belt.

Practice 1

In the following sentences, insert commas between items in a series.

1. Most communities now recycle newspapers aluminum and plastic.

2. Walking bicycling and swimming are all good aerobic exercises.

3. We collected the kids loaded the van and set off for the amusement park.

4. Signs of burnout include insomnia inability to concentrate and depression.

2 AFTER INTRODUCTORY MATERIAL

A comma is used to separate introductory material from the rest of the sentence. (If you were reading the sentence aloud, you would probably pause slightly at the end of the introductory material, where the comma belongs.)

> Although the county issues a large number of jury-duty notices, many people find reasons not to serve.
>
> Pushing and laughing, the second-graders spilled onto the playground.
>
> In the middle of the thunderstorm, all the lights on our street went out.

Practice 2

Insert a comma after the introductory material in each of the following sentences.

1. During the first-aid course one student accidentally broke her finger.

2. When the power went back on all the digital clocks in the house began to blink.

3. Pausing in the doorway the actress smiled warmly at the photographers.

4. After waiting in line for two hours the students were told that the registrar's office was closing for lunch.

3 AROUND WORDS THAT INTERRUPT THE FLOW OF A SENTENCE

Sentences sometimes contain words (often called **parenthetical expressions**) that interrupt the flow of thought. Such words and word groups should be set off from the rest of the sentence by commas. For example,

Someone's car, a blue Ford, was blocking the store entrance.

If you read this sentence out loud, you can hear that the words *a blue Ford* interrupt the flow of thought. (This type of interrupter, a noun that means the same as the noun before it, is called an **appositive**.) Such interrupters often contain information that is less important to the sentence.

Here are some other examples of sentences with interrupters:

The owner of the blue Ford, *grumbling angrily,* came out to move his car.

Our house, *which was built in 1975,* needs a new roof and extra insulation.

The house's storm windows, *though,* are in fairly good shape.

Note   Some interrupters, however, are needed to make the sentence clear. Information about punctuating these word groups appears on page 212.

Practice 3

Insert commas around the interrupting words in each of the following sentences.

1. The Beatles who originally called themselves the Quarrymen released twenty-nine single records in their first year.

2. Frozen yogurt a dessert that is relatively low in calories is as delicious to many people as ice cream.

3. Some dieters on the other hand would rather give up desserts completely.

4. The new office building forty stories high provides a fine view of the parkway.

4 BETWEEN COMPLETE THOUGHTS CONNECTED BY A JOINING WORD

When two complete thoughts are combined into one sentence by a joining word like *and, but,* or *so,* a comma is used before the joining word.

They were five strangers stuck in an elevator, **so** they told each other jokes to ease the tension.

Each part of the sentence is a complete thought: *They were five strangers stuck in an elevator. They told each other jokes to ease the tension.* The parts are combined into one sentence by the joining word *so.*

Here are more sentences with complete thoughts connected by joining words:

Money may not buy happiness, **but** it makes misery a lot more comfortable.

Ved has a restaurant job this summer, **and** his sister has an office position.

Punctuation note   Don't add a comma just because a sentence contains the word *and, but,* or *so.* Use a comma only when the joining word comes between two complete thoughts. Each of those thoughts must have its own subject and verb.

> *Comma:* Lois spent two hours in the *gym,* **and then she went** to class. (Each complete thought has a subject and a verb: *Lois spent* and *she went.*)
>
> *No comma:* Lois spent two hours in the **gym and then went** to class. (The second thought isn't complete because it doesn't have its own subject.)

Practice 4

Insert a comma before the joining words in the following sentences.

1. The horror-movie heroine screamed for help but nobody heard her.

2. Melba wasn't wearing her glasses so she couldn't read the fine print in the ad.

3. I used to be able to type very quickly but now I'm out of practice.

4. Frequent TV watchers spend less time interacting with friends and family and their reading is often limited to magazines such as *TV Guide.*

5 WITH DIRECT QUOTATIONS

A comma is used to separate directly quoted material from the rest of the sentence.

> Someone shouted**,** "Look out below!"
>
> The customer grumbled to the waiter**,** "This coffee tastes like mud."
>
> "To learn more about lions," the zookeeper told the visiting children**,** "you should read the book *Born Free.*"

Punctuation note   When the comma is placed at the end of a quotation, it is included within the quotation marks.

Practice 5

Insert commas to set off quoted material in the following sentences.

1. When the bank robber Willie Sutton was asked why he robbed banks, he replied "Because that's where the money is."

2. "Only fifteen more minutes until this class ends" Sharon whispered.

3. "We have everything for tall women" the mall store owner bragged "except tall men."

4. "When you hear the beep, you know what to do" says the message on my friend's answering machine.

Note   Additional information about the comma appears on pages 212–215.

Name _____ Section _____ Date _____

■ ## Comma: Test 1

On the lines provided, write the word or words in each sentence that need to be followed by a comma. Be sure to include each comma.

Note   To help you master the comma, explanations are given for five of the sentences.

1. The kids' Halloween bags were full of quarters peanuts gum and candy bars.

   _____   Commas separate items in a series.

2. Opal has evening classes on Mondays Wednesdays and Thursdays.

   _____

3. Carrying her popcorn Sylvia looked for an empty seat in the theater.

   _____   Use a comma after introductory material.

4. After she read the Harry Potter books Yoko began calling her younger brothers and sisters "Muggles."

   _____

5. That pizza the one with broccoli and mushrooms is the best I've ever eaten.

   _____   Place commas around interrupting words in a sentence.

6. I ate Rocky Road ice cream which is not on my diet for dinner last night.

   _____

7. My father wanted to attend college but his family didn't have the money.

   _____   A comma is needed before the word that joins two complete thoughts.

8. Bad weather destroyed much of last season's orange crop so the price of orange juice is high this year.

   _____

9. "You look as if you've seen a ghost" my brother remarked when he saw the scared expression on my face.

   _____   The comma separates a direct quotation from the rest of the sentence.

10. "All I want" said Jeff wearily "is to crawl into bed and stay there for a week."

   _____

Name _____ Section _____ Date _____

Score: (Number right) _____ × 10 = _____ %

■ Comma: Test 2

In the space provided, write the letter of the one comma rule that applies to each of the following sentences. Then insert one or more commas where they belong in each sentence.

a	Between items in a series
b	After introductory material
c	Around interrupting words
d	Before a word that joins two complete thoughts
e	With direct quotations

_____ 1. The caged panther which kept striding from one side of its enclosure to the other looked both magnificent and pitiful.

_____ 2. When I first picked up the telephone I didn't recognize Roger's voice.

_____ 3. You'll know my uncle immediately—he has a walrus mustache an eye patch and a wooden leg.

_____ 4. I'm glad my little niece loves the ocean but she really needs to learn how to swim.

_____ 5. "I'll go to the party" said Vicky "if you promise to be there."

_____ 6. Many parents although they dearly love their children sometimes dream about being young and free again.

_____ 7. Being educated doesn't mean having a head full of facts but it does mean knowing how and where to find the facts.

_____ 8. The insensitive TV reporter shouted to his camera crew "Make sure you get some close-ups of the accident victims!"

_____ 9. The supermarket is having specials this week on ground beef coffee and cereal.

_____ 10. On the other hand the store has raised its prices on fish and milk.

Name _____   Section _____ Date _____

Score: (Number right) _____ × 10 = _____%

■ Comma: Test 3

On the lines provided, write out the parts of each passage that need commas. Be sure to include the commas.

Note   To help you master the comma, explanations are given for half of the corrections.

1. The principal announced in a loud voice "Please welcome our graduates!" The graduating class wearing royal blue caps and gowns then marched into the auditorium.

   a. _____
   A comma is needed to separate quoted words from the rest of the sentence.

   b. _____

2. My psychology class is very practical. We've learned about causes of stress everyday defense mechanisms and coping skills. In addition I now understand a good deal about the anger I have toward my parents.

   a. _____
   Commas are needed to separate the items in a series.

   b. _____

3. A fire siren outside woke Kim at 5:30 so she got dressed and went for an early morning run. "You're up bright and early" a neighbor called to her.

   a. _____
   Put a comma before the word that joins two complete thoughts.

   b. _____

4. Alvin who weighs 260 pounds works as a bouncer in a nightclub. When he tells people it's time to leave few of them argue with Alvin.

   a. _____
   Commas are needed around the words that interrupt the first sentence.

   b. _____

5. Home from his first day at kindergarten the little boy stumbled into the house. He dropped his brightly colored book bag on the floor collapsed on the couch and promptly fell asleep.

   a. _____
   Put a comma after the introductory words.

   b. _____

Name _____ Section _____ Date _____

Score: (Number right) _____ × 10 = _____ %

■ Comma: Test 4

On the lines provided, write out the parts of each passage that need commas. Be sure to include the commas.

1. The trees especially the newly planted maples were badly damaged by the construction trucks. Broken branches oozing bark and wilted leaves were all signs that the trees might die.

   a. _____

   b. _____

2. "I just hate what's happened to the Sunday paper" Mel said. "The comics section my favorite part is now in small print and hidden inside the TV listings."

   a. _____

   b. _____

3. My eighteen-year-old brother's dream is an apartment of his own a new Corvette with racing stripes and a beautiful girlfriend with a good job. Although I think he's hopelessly unrealistic I don't want to be the one to discourage him.

   a. _____

   b. _____

4. P. T. Barnum the master showman once hitched an elephant to a plow in order to promote his circus. As a result it is still a crime in North Carolina to plow a field with an elephant.

   a. _____

   b. _____

5. Early in the twentieth century women did not have the right to vote. That was not the only injustice experienced by women. Many people thought that higher education was wasted on women so very few women had the opportunity to attend college.

   a. _____

   b. _____

Name _____ Section _____ Date _____

Score: (Number right) _____ × 10 = _____%

■ Comma: Test 5

On the lines provided, write the word or words in each sentence that need to be followed by a comma. Be sure to include the commas. One comma rule applies in each sentence.

Note   To help you master the comma, explanations are given for five of the sentences.

[1]Most of us probably think that "reality television" which features ordinary people in unscripted situations is a 21st-century phenomenon. [2]The truth is that this kind of programming is not new for it actually began more than sixty years ago. [3]Today's reality TV programs can be traced back to the hidden-camera programs game shows and talent competitions of the 1940s and 1950s. [4]Allen Funt the creator and original host of *Candid Camera* would set up unusual situations and film people without their knowledge. [5]Then he would say "Smile! You're on *Candid Camera*." [6]*Candid Camera* originally broadcast in 1948 is considered the first reality TV show and the ancestor of recent programs like *Punk'd*. [7]Thanks to the 1950s game show *Beat the Clock* we now have such "elimination" shows as *The Amazing Race* and *Survivor*. [8]Beginning with *American Idol* in 2002 talent competitions have become quite popular. [9]Few people today remember *Ted Mack's Original Amateur Hour* or *Arthur Godfrey's Talent Scouts* but both of these 1948 shows also had amateur contestants and audience voting. [10]Because reality shows have been popular for such a long time we will probably see even more of them in future seasons.

1. _____
   Use commas around interrupting words in a sentence.

2. _____

3. _____
   Use commas to separate items in a series.

4. _____

5. _____
   Use a comma to separate quoted words from the rest of the sentence.

6. _____

7. _____
   Use a comma after introductory material.

8. _____

9. _____
   Use a comma before a word that joins two complete thoughts.

10. _____

■ Comma: Test 6

On the lines provided, write the word or words in each sentence that need to be followed by a comma. Be sure to include the commas. One comma rule applies in each sentence.

[1]I love old-fashioned horror films that feature vampires werewolves mummies and zombies. [2]The monster movie I love best of all is *Frankenstein* but it was only recently that I read the original book by that name. [3]I was surprised to learn that its author Mary Shelley was very young. [4]The daughter of scholars Mary was an intelligent and talented young woman. [5]She eloped at seventeen with Percy Shelley a well-known poet and traveled to Switzerland. [6]In Switzerland, their party included Mary her husband another poet (Lord Byron) and Byron's physician. [7]Someone in the group said "Let's each write a story about the supernatural." [8]Mary's contribution a story about a living creature made from dead bodies was *Frankenstein*. [9]The story published when Mary was twenty-one years old became an instant classic. [10]Because of its wide appeal it has been the subject of many movies—and nightmares.

1. _____

2. _____

3. _____

4. _____

5. _____

6. _____

7. _____

8. _____

9. _____

10. _____

9 Apostrophe

Seeing What You Know

Insert apostrophes where needed in the four sentences below. Then read the explanations that follow.

1. Its impossible for water to run uphill.

2. The prosecutor cant try any new cases until next month.

3. No one likes the registrars new procedures for dropping a course.

4. The omelets at the Greens diner are the best in town. Mrs. Green is the chef, and her husband is the host.

Understanding the Answers

1. **It's** impossible for water to run uphill.

   It's is the contraction of the words *it is*. The apostrophe takes the place of the letter *i*, which has been left out.

2. The prosecutor **can't** try any new cases until next month.

   Can't is the contraction of the words *can not*. The apostrophe shows that two letters, *n* and *o*, have been left out.

3. No one likes the **registrar's** new procedures for dropping a course.

   The apostrophe plus *s* shows that the new procedures belong to the registrar. The apostrophe goes after the last letter of *registrar. Likes* does not get an apostrophe; it is a verb. *Procedures* also does not get an apostrophe, because it is not possessive. It is a plural word meaning "more than one procedure."

4. The omelets at the **Greens'** diner are the best in town. Mrs. Green is the chef, and her husband is the host.

   The apostrophe after the *s* shows that the Greens own the diner. With possessive plural words ending in *s*, the apostrophe alone shows possession. *Omelets* does not need an apostrophe, because it is simply a plural word meaning "more than one omelet."

The apostrophe is a punctuation mark with two main purposes. It is used in a **contraction** to show that one or more letters have been left out of a word. The apostrophe is also used to show **possession**—that is, to show that something belongs to someone or something.

APOSTROPHE IN CONTRACTIONS

A contraction is formed when two words are combined to make a new word. The apostrophe takes the place of the letter or letters omitted in forming the contraction. It goes where the missing letters used to be.

Here are a few common contractions:

I + am = **I'm** (the letter *a* in *am* has been left out)

it + is = **it's** (the *i* in *is* has been left out)

does + not = **doesn't** (the *o* in *not* has been left out)

do + not = **don't** (the *o* in *not* has been left out)

she + will = **she'll** (the *wi* in *will* has been left out)

you + would = **you'd** (the *woul* in *would* has been left out)

will + not = **won't** (*o* takes the place of *ill;* the *o* in *not* has been left out)

Contractions are commonly used in everyday speech and writing, as seen in this passage:

Let's go to the movies tonight. *There's* a film *I've* been wanting to see, but it *hasn't* been in town until now. *Didn't* you say *you've* been wanting to see it too? *Shouldn't* we ask Michael and Ana to go with us? *They're* always ready to see a good film. And they *don't* have anything to do this evening.

Practice 1

In the spaces provided, write the contractions of the words in parentheses.

1. *(What is)* _____ the best reality show *(that is)* _____ on TV this season?

2. When the timer goes off, *(you will)* _____ know *(it is)* _____ time to take the potatoes out of the microwave.

3. *(I would)* _____ like to speak to the person *(who is)* _____ in charge of the shoe department.

4. It *(is not)* _____ fair that some companies *(are not)* _____ hiring older workers.

5. The game show contestants *(did not)* _____ win the trip to Hawaii, but

   (they are) _____ getting a box of pineapples as a consolation prize.

Four Confusing Pairs

Four contractions that can cause problems are *they're* (meaning *they are*), *it's* (meaning *it is* or *it has*), *you're* (meaning *you are*), and *who's* (meaning *who is*). They are easily confused with the possessive forms *their* (meaning *belonging to them*), *its* (meaning *belonging to it*), *your* (meaning *belonging to you*), and *whose* (meaning *belonging to whom*). Notice how each of these words is used in the sentences below:

They're *(they are)* very angry about the damage done to **their** new mailbox *(the new mailbox belonging to them)*.

It's *(it is)* a shame that your car has blown **its** engine *(the engine belonging to it)*.

Your parents *(the parents belonging to you)* said that **you're** *(you are)* supposed to be home by midnight.

Who's *(who is)* the person **whose** car *(the car belonging to whom)* is taking up two parking spaces?

Practice 2

Underline the correct word in each set of parentheses.

1. (It's, Its) too late now to give the dog (it's, its) bath.
2. Have Matt and Sara told (they're, their) parents that (they're, their) planning to start their own business?
3. (Who's, Whose) going to tell me (who's, whose) drink this is?
4. I think that (you're, your) best quality is (you're, your) sense of humor.
5. (It's, Its) revealing that only four pieces of United States currency have had women's pictures on (they're, their) front or back sides. The women (who's, whose) faces have been on U.S. money are Martha Washington, Pocahontas, Susan B. Anthony, and Sacajawea. What's (your, you're) guess as to why these four women were chosen?

THE APOSTROPHE TO SHOW POSSESSION

To show that something belongs to someone or something, we could say, for example, *the truck owned by Sally, the radial tires belonging to the car,* or *the Great Dane of the neighbor.* But it's much simpler to say the following:

Sally's truck

the car's radial tires

the neighbor's Great Dane

To make a singular word (or a plural word not ending in *s*) possessive, add an apostrophe plus an *s*. To decide *what* to make possessive, ask yourself the following:

1   Who or what is owned?

2   Who or what owns something?

Then put the apostrophe plus an *s* after the name of the owner.
      For example, look at the following word group:

      the truck owned by Sally

First ask yourself, "What is owned?" The answer is *the truck.* Then ask, "Who is the owner?" The answer is *Sally.* So add an apostrophe plus *s* after the name of the owner: *Sally's truck.* The apostrophe plus *s* shows that the truck belongs to Sally.
      Here is another example:

      the toys belonging to the children

Again, ask yourself, "What is owned?" The answer is *toys.* Then ask, "Who is the owner?" The answer is *the children.* So add an apostrophe plus *s* after the name of the owner: *the children's toys.* The apostrophe plus *s* shows that the toys belong to the children.

Notes

1   An apostrophe plus *s* is used to show possession, even with a singular word that already ends in *s:*

Tess**'s** purse (the purse belonging to Tess)

the boss**'s** car (the car owned by the boss)

2   But an apostrophe alone is used to show possession with a plural word that ends in *s:*

several students**'** complaints (the complaints of several students)

the two teams**'** agreement (the agreement of the two teams)

Practice 3

Two apostrophes are needed to show possession in each sentence below. In each space provided, write the word or words that need the apostrophe (the owner) as well as what is owned. The first sentence is done for you as an example.

1. The spiders web glistened with moisture from last nights rain.

      _____ spider's web _____   _____ last night's rain _____

2. The mail carriers job is not made any easier by that mans vicious dog.

      _____   _____

3. Everyones assignment is to prepare a two-minute speech for Mondays class.

      _____   _____

4. Ben Franklins inventions were often a combination of other peoples ideas.

_____   _____

5. Doriss grades are better than both of her brothers grades ever were.

_____   _____

When Not to Use an Apostrophe: In Plurals and Verbs

People sometimes confuse possessive and plural forms of words. Remember that a plural is formed simply by adding an *s* to a word; no apostrophe is used. Look at the sentence below to see which words are plural and which are possessive:

Tina's new boots have silver buckles.

The words *boots* and *buckles* are plurals—there is more than one boot, and there is more than one buckle. But *Tina's*, the word with the apostrophe plus *s*, is possessive. Tina owns the boots.

Also, many verbs end with just an *s*—for example, the word *owns* in the sentence "Tina owns the boots." Do not put an apostrophe in a verb.

Practice 4

In the spaces provided under each sentence, add the one apostrophe needed and explain why the other words ending in *s* do not get apostrophes.

Example   The little boys daily temper tantrum seems to last for hours.

boys: _boy's, meaning "belonging to the little boy"_

seems: _verb_

hours: _plural meaning "more than one hour"_

1. Lucys boyfriend sends her over twenty text messages a day.

   Lucys: _____

   messages: _____

2. That old storefronts grimy window has not been cleaned in many years.

   storefronts: _____

   years: _____

3. The managers mood is much better after she gives out the assignments for the day.

   managers: _____

   gives: _____

   assignments: _____

4. This years new television shows are much worse than the programs of past seasons.

   years: _____

   shows: _____

   programs: _____

   seasons: _____

5. The motor of our sons old car coughs and wheezes whenever it starts.

   sons: _____

   coughs: _____

   wheezes: _____

   starts: _____

6. One of Theos failings is jumping to conclusions.

   Theos: _____

   failings: _____

   conclusions: _____

7. Dieters should drink eight glasses of water a day because of waters ability to make the stomach feel more full.

   Dieters: _____

   glasses: _____

   waters: _____

8. On the game reserve, dozens of elephants crowded around the two water holes edges.

   dozens: _____

   elephants: _____

   water holes: _____

   edges: _____

Note   Additional information about the apostrophe appears on page 216.

Name _____ Section _____ Date _____

■ Apostrophe: Test 1

Each of the sentences below contains one word that needs an apostrophe. Write each word, with its apostrophe, in the space provided.

Note   To help you master the apostrophe, explanations are given for half of the sentences.

1. The teachers broken leg kept her out of class for two weeks.

    _____   The broken leg belongs to the teacher.
                                    Weeks is plural.

2. That insurance companys best customers are construction workers.

    _____

3. Im taking extra courses so I can graduate one semester early.

    _____   An apostrophe should take the place of the
                                    missing *a* in the contraction.

4. The students know that they cant fool Mrs. Striker with phony excuses.

    _____

5. The huge green frogs sticky tongue soon captured several flies.

    _____   The frog owns the sticky tongue. *Flies* is a
                                    simple plural.

6. Endorphins, the bodys natural painkillers, are released when people exercise.

    _____

7. A sign in front of the store entrance says, "Dont even *think* of parking here!"

    _____   *Don't* is a contraction of *do not,* with the *o* in
                                    not left out. *Says* is a verb.

8. Its supposed to rain for the next three days, so we can skip watering the lawn.

    _____

9. A tornado destroyed the barns roof, but no animals were killed.

    _____   The roof belongs to the barn. *Animals* is a
                                    simple plural.

10. Even though they live a thousand miles apart, the two brothers relationship
    has remained strong through the years.

    _____

Name _____ Section _____ Date _____

Score: (Number right) _____ × 10 = _____%

■ Apostrophe: Test 2

Each of the sentences below contains one word that needs an apostrophe. Write each word, with its apostrophe, in the space provided.

1. Because I had a lot of e-mails to answer, I didnt get to sleep until 2 a.m.

   _____

2. According to many scientists, the shrinking of Earths ozone layer will result in rising temperatures.

   _____

3. When the ballparks gates opened, hundreds of fans were already waiting outside.

   _____

4. Many of the streets residents have lived there for at least twenty years.

   _____

5. If the canary hasnt eaten its food by morning, you should take the canary to the veterinarian.

   _____

6. Babysitters dont usually agree to take care of those twins a second time.

   _____

7. More than one-fourth of the librarys books are missing from the shelves.

   _____

8. My grandmothers hairdo looks the same today as it did when she was twenty.

   _____

9. I went to the post office, but its open only until noon on Saturdays.

   _____

10. Ramona couldnt start either of her cars, so she had to call a tow truck.

    _____

Name _____   Section _____   Date _____

Score: (Number right) _____ × 10 = _____ %

■ **Apostrophe: Test 3**

Each of the short passages below contains two words that need apostrophes. Underline the words that need apostrophes. Then write each word, with its apostrophe, in the space provided.

Note   To help you master the apostrophe, explanations are given for the first sentence in each passage.

1. Gregs jeans should go into the ragbag. Theyve got to be at least fifteen years old.

   a. _____   The jeans belong to Greg.

   b. _____

2. Whos the person in charge of repairs around here? The copy machines red light is flashing again.

   a. _____   An apostrophe should take the place of the

   b. _____   missing *i* in the contraction.

3. "Im surprised that you take my grades so seriously," said Ned to his father. "Grades are no measure of a persons true worth."

   a. _____   An apostrophe should take the place of the

   b. _____   missing *a* in the contraction.

4. Kates tights began to slip down to her knees as she walked back from the school stage. She couldnt do anything about it, so she kept her head down and hoped nobody would notice.

   a. _____   The tights belong to Kate.

   b. _____

5. A tiny crack appeared in the fish tanks corner. The goldfish looked unconcerned, but their owner didnt feel as calm.

   a. _____   The corner belongs to the fish tank.

   b. _____

■ Apostrophe: Test 4

Each of the short passages below contains two words that need apostrophes. Underline the words that need apostrophes. Then write each word, with its apostrophe, in the space provided.

1. Just as I finished typing my paper, my computers hard drive crashed. Fortunately, I had backed up the papers previous draft on a flash drive.

   a. _____

   b. _____

2. The books cover shows a beautiful woman and a handsome man in each others arms. That is odd, because the book is not a love story at all.

   a. _____

   b. _____

3. "Ricks sneakers are in the middle of the kitchen floor," his father said. "So hes sure to be around here somewhere."

   a. _____

   b. _____

4. Some peoples lack of consideration is beyond belief. Our neighbors, for example, have parties every Saturday night where they sing and play loud music until dawn. And they havent invited us to a single one.

   a. _____

   b. _____

5. "Youre not thinking of asking me for my car keys again, are you?" Ivan said to his sixteen-year-old daughter. "Getting a drivers license does not mean you automatically get a car to go with it."

   a. _____

   b. _____

Name _____   Section _____   Date _____

Score: (Number right) _____ × 10 = _____ %

■ Apostrophe: Test 5

Each sentence in the following passage contains a word that requires an apostrophe. Underline the ten words. Then, on the lines following the passage, write the corrected form of each word.

Note   To help you master the apostrophe, explanations are given for five of the sentences.

[1]In this paragraph youre likely to learn something new about President Barack Obama. [2]As a six-year-old child in Indonesia, he ate grasshopper, dog meat, and snake meat, which are not among Indonesias main dishes. [3]His classmates nickname for him, which he used until college, was "Barry." [4]His familys pets included birds, a dog, two baby crocodiles, and an ape named Tata. [5]At age ten, Barack moved back to Hawaii to live with his grandparents and attended Honolulus prestigious Punahou School. [6]Ever since working at Baskin-Robbins as a teenager, he hasnt liked ice cream. [7]In 2006, Obama won a Grammy Award for a voice recording of his first book, *Dreams from My Father,* which is about Obamas search for his identity. [8]Obama plays basketball, and soon after the election, he said that hed install a basketball court on the White House grounds. [9]During his presidential campaign, he watched sports regularly but didnt watch the news very much. [10]Barack Obama has become one of the worlds most respected figures since being elected the first African-American president of the United States.

1. _____   The contraction of *you are* needs an apostrophe.

2. _____

3. _____   The nickname was used by his classmates, so the plural possessive is needed.

4. _____

5. _____   Punahou School belongs to the city of Honolulu.

6. _____

7. _____   The search belonged to Obama.

8. _____

9. _____   The contraction of *did not* needs an apostrophe.

10. _____

Name _____ Section _____ Date _____

Score: (Number right) _____ × 10 = _____%

■ Apostrophe: Test 6

Each sentence in the following passage contains a word that requires an apostrophe. Underline the ten words. Then, on the lines following the passage, write the corrected form of each word.

¹One of historys most fascinating figures is Cleopatra, a queen of ancient Egypt. ²She was born in the year 69 B.C., and in keeping with one of the ancient Egyptian traditions, she became her brothers wife when she was made queen. ³Her brother soon drove her from Egypts throne, however, and she began making plans to go to war against him. ⁴When Cleopatras beauty and charm caught the eye of the Roman general Julius Caesar, they became lovers. ⁵Caesars feelings for Cleopatra were so strong that he went to war for her, killing her brother. ⁶She became queen again, marrying a younger brother, but it wasnt long before she poisoned her new husband. ⁷Later on, Caesar was murdered, and Cleopatra became the mistress of one of Romes most powerful military figures, Mark Antony. ⁸But when Antonys soldiers were defeated in battle, Cleopatra agreed to join the plot of an enemy, Octavian, by pretending to commit suicide. ⁹Antony didnt want to live without her, so he killed himself. ¹⁰When she couldnt persuade Octavian to become her lover and ally, Cleopatra put an end to her own violent life.

1. _____

2. _____

3. _____

4. _____

5. _____

6. _____

7. _____

8. _____

9. _____

10. _____

10 Quotation Marks

Seeing What You Know

Insert quotation marks or underlines as needed in the following sentences. One sentence does not need quotation marks. Then read the explanations below.

1. The mechanic said, Your car needs more than a tune-up.

2. To tell you the truth, said my husband, I'm thinking of quitting my job.

3. My sister called to say that she needed heart surgery.

4. According to The Book of Answers, the most widely sung song in the English-speaking world is Happy Birthday to You.

Understanding the Answers

1. The mechanic said, "Your car needs more than a tune-up."
   The words *Your car needs more than a tune-up* need quotation marks. These are the exact words that the mechanic said. Since *Your* is the first word of a quoted sentence, it is capitalized.

2. "To tell you the truth," said my husband, "I'm thinking of quitting my job."
   Each of the two word groups spoken by the husband, since they are his exact words, needs a set of quotation marks.

3. My sister called to say that she needed heart surgery.
   The words *that she needed heart surgery* are not the speaker's exact words. (Her exact words would have been "I need heart surgery.") In such an indirect quotation, no quotation marks are used.

4. According to <u>The Book of Answers</u>, the most widely sung song in the English-speaking world is "Happy Birthday to You."
   Titles of short works, such as songs, are put in quotation marks. Titles of longer works, such as books, are either italicized or underlined.

Quotation marks enclose the exact words of a speaker or writer. Quotation marks also set off the title of a short work.

QUOTATION MARKS TO SET OFF THE WORDS OF A SPEAKER OR WRITER

Use quotation marks to set off the exact words of a speaker or writer.

> After the bombing of Pearl Harbor, President Franklin Roosevelt described the day as "a date which will live in infamy."
> (President Roosevelt's exact words are enclosed in quotation marks.)

> "When we're done with the dishes," said Terry, "we'll be ready to go."
> (Terry's exact words are set off by two sets of quotation marks. The words *said Terry* are not included in the quotation marks since they were not spoken by him.)

> Opal told her uncle, "We'll serve dinner at seven o'clock. If you can't make it then, stop in later for dessert."
> (Because the two sentences give Opal's words without interruption, they require just one set of quotation marks.)

> "Experience," wrote Vernon Law, "is a hard teacher because she gives the test first, the lesson afterward."
> (The exact words that Law wrote are enclosed in quotation marks.)

Punctuation note   Quoted material is usually set off from the rest of the sentence by a comma. When the comma comes at the end of quoted material, it is included inside the quotation marks. The same is true for a period, exclamation point, or question mark that ends quoted material:

Incorrect:	"If it rains", said Connie, "the ball game will be canceled".
Correct:	"If it rains," said Connie, "the ball game will be canceled."

Notice, too, that a quoted sentence begins with a capital letter, even when it is preceded by other words.

Incorrect:	Marco said, "let's go to the fair tonight."
Correct:	Marco said, "Let's go to the fair tonight."

Practice 1

Insert quotation marks where needed.

1. My throat is so sore I can't talk, Larry whispered.

2. Wilson Mizner once said, Life's a tough proposition, and the first hundred years are the hardest.

Name _____   Section _____   Date _____

■ Quotation Marks: Test 3

Place quotation marks where needed in the short passages that follow. Each passage needs **two** sets of quotation marks.

Note   To help you master quotation marks, explanations are given for one set of quotation marks in each passage.

1. May I ask you a personal question? asked my nosy neighbor, as if she needed my permission. You may ask it, but I probably won't answer it, I replied.
   The neighbor's question should be set off with one set of quotation marks.

2. Benjamin Franklin is famous for his witty sayings. Many of them give advice on how to behave; others are comments on human nature. For instance, he once wrote, To lengthen thy life, lessen thy meals. He also commented, Three may keep a secret, if two of them are dead.
   Franklin's advice on behavior should be set off with one set of quotation marks.

3. When Mr. Benton asked to withdraw some money from his account, the bank teller said, I'm sorry, but your account is overdrawn. Mr. Benton answered, Nonsense, I must still have money in my account. See, I have lots of checks left.
   The teller's words should be set off with quotation marks.

4. I asked James how, if he couldn't find his shoes, he expected to get dressed for the wedding. I could always wear my sneakers, he answered. We'll have to sit in back where nobody sees us, then, I told him.
   James's exact words should be set off with one set of quotation marks.

5. This article titled How to Find Your Perfect Mate in *Cosmopolitan* is the dumbest thing I've ever read. It actually suggests that before you go on a first date, you ask your date, Please fill out this questionnaire on your likes and dislikes.
   The title of an article is put in quotation marks.

Name _____   Section _____   Date _____
Score: (Number right) _____ × 10 = _____ %

■ Quotation Marks: Test 4

Place quotation marks where needed in the short passages that follow. Each passage needs **two** sets of quotation marks.

1. Lights out right now! my mother shouted up the stairs. The lights were turned off, but a great deal of noise and giggling ensued. Mother waited patiently for things to quiet a bit and then called up, You'll be too tired for school tomorrow if you don't get to sleep.

2. An angry-looking woman marched up to the customer service desk and slammed a large box on the counter. You sold me this juicer, and now I want my money back, she told the clerk. Every time I turn it on, it spits carrot pieces all over my kitchen table.

3. The interviewer poked her head out of the office door and called out, Please come in, Mr. Ortiz. She asked him a few questions about his education and job history. Then she said, You're the twentieth applicant for this position. Please tell me why I should hire you instead of any of the others.

4. Hey, you, called the homeless man sitting on the sidewalk. A well-dressed young man paused. Are you talking to me? he asked.

5. You bet I am. How would you like to trade places with me? said the homeless man. The young man smiled nervously and then said that he would prefer not to. The older man nodded. I don't blame you, he said and lay back down on the pavement.

Name _____ Section _____ Date _____

Score: (Number right) _____ × 10 = _____%

■ Quotation Marks: Test 5

Ten of the sentences in the passage below require a set of quotation marks. Insert the quotation marks where needed. On the lines provided at the bottom, write the numbers of the sentences to which you have added quotation marks.

Note   To help you master quotation marks, five of the sentences that need quotation marks are identified for you.

¹Last summer I went with my husband Lenny to his ten-year high school reunion. ²He kept telling me, Oh, boy, are you going to love my old gang. ³I'd heard a lot about the old gang, and I wondered about that. ⁴Not only are we going to have a great time, but I'm going to be master of ceremonies, he announced.

⁵On the big night, we'd barely driven into the parking lot when we were surrounded by a crowd of apparently grown men shouting, Li-zard! Li-zard! Lenny the Lizard has arrived! ⁶I turned and looked at my husband. ⁷Lenny the Lizard? I asked. ⁸He didn't have time to answer. ⁹Party time! he roared, leaping out of the car and disappearing into the building.

¹⁰When I caught up with him, he was being hugged and kissed by a good-looking redhead. ¹¹Ooooohhhh, she said, looking me over. ¹²You sure don't look like the type that Lenny would have married!

¹³After a year or so we sat down to dinner. ¹⁴There, people kept saying things like Do you remember the time Jock dissected the frog and gave its heart to Diane on Valentine's Day? ¹⁵Everybody at the table would break up laughing at that point, while I was still waiting to hear what had happened.

¹⁶Finally it was time for Lenny to get up and speak. ¹⁷He actually did a pretty good job, and he finished his remarks by asking the class members to introduce their spouses. ¹⁸To get things started, he had me stand as he said, And this is my wonderful wife, Betty. ¹⁹Unfortunately, my name is Linda.

²⁰When it's time for Lenny's twentieth, I'm going to stay home and write an article called Surviving Your Spouse's Reunion.

1. Sentence __2__   6. Sentence ____

2. Sentence ____   7. Sentence __12__

3. Sentence __5__   8. Sentence ____

4. Sentence ____   9. Sentence __18__

5. Sentence __9__   10. Sentence ____

Name _____   Section _____   Date _____

Score: (Number right) _____ × 10 = _____%

■ Quotation Marks: Test 6

Ten of the sentences in the passage below require a set of quotation marks. Insert the quotation marks where needed. On the lines provided at the bottom, write the numbers of the sentences to which you have added quotation marks.

¹Last summer, I went on a road trip with my best friend, Lindsay. ²Since we had read an article titled The Majesty of the Grand Canyon, we were both eager to see this natural wonder. ³We left from Indiana and drove out west, stopping in Colorado to visit some friends from college. ⁴You're going to love Colorado in the summer! our friend Jamie kept telling us before we arrived. ⁵We planned on staying there for two days before continuing on our trip.

⁶Two weeks later, we were still in Colorado. ⁷I have a free pass for white water rafting, Jamie said. ⁸I'll take you horseback riding, our friend Brian told us. ⁹Would you like to go hiking on the trails behind our house? Bethany asked. ¹⁰When Jamie told us that she could get us tickets to a concert, we decided we would never leave. ¹¹Everyone was so nice, and there were so many enjoyable things to do.

¹²Eventually, we found ourselves driving out of Colorado and then through Utah. ¹³As we drove through the Utah deserts, Lindsay commented, I can't believe how different it is out here. ¹⁴We stared in awe at the gigantic red rocks all around us. ¹⁵Just wait until you see the Grand Canyon! I replied.

¹⁶Several hours later, we were driving at night. ¹⁷Wow! Lindsay said. ¹⁸What is *that*? ¹⁹I looked ahead and saw a massive row of twinkling lights over the dark horizon. ²⁰I think it's Las Vegas, I said as I realized we had taken a wrong turn and had missed Arizona. ²¹We drove into Las Vegas, deciding to visit the Grand Canyon on another trip.

1. Sentence ____   6. Sentence ____

2. Sentence ____   7. Sentence ____

3. Sentence ____   8. Sentence ____

4. Sentence ____   9. Sentence ____

5. Sentence ____   10. Sentence ____

11 Other Punctuation Marks

Seeing What You Know

Add a period, a question mark, or an exclamation mark to each sentence that follows. Use a different end mark in each sentence. Then read the explanations below.

1. Half of all the people in America live in just eight of the fifty states

2. Are you going to the high school reunion

3. Stop that noise before I go crazy

Insert a colon, a semicolon, and parentheses where needed in the following sentences.

4. Rocky Road my favorite ice cream flavor contains marshmallows and nuts.

5. The bearded man looked around the quiet bank then he passed the teller a folded note. Two emotions showed on the teller's face surprise and terror.

Insert a hyphen and dashes where needed in the following sentence.

6. Nobody not even her attorney believed the woman's odd sounding alibi.

Understanding the Answers

1. states.   2. reunion?   3. crazy!

   Sentence 1 makes a statement, so a period is needed. Sentence 2 asks a question and so must end with a question mark. Sentence 3 expresses strong feeling, so an exclamation point is appropriate.

4. (my favorite ice cream flavor)

   The parentheses set off information that is not essential to the rest of the sentence.

5. bank; then . . . face: surprise

   The semicolon connects two complete thoughts, each with its own subject and verb. The colon introduces an explanation of the idea stated just before the colon.

6. Nobody—not even her attorney—believed . . . odd-sounding alibi.

   Dashes emphasize the words *not even her attorney*. A hyphen joins the two words that act together to describe the noun *alibi*.

This chapter first describes three marks of punctuation that are used to end a sentence: the period (.), the question mark (?), and the exclamation point (!). The chapter then describes five additional marks of punctuation: the colon (:), semi-colon (;), hyphen (-), dash (—), and parentheses ( ).

PERIOD (.)

Use a period at the end of a statement, a mild command, or an indirect question.

> Only the female mosquito drinks blood.
>
> Go let the dog out.
>
> I wonder if it's going to rain.

The period is also used at the end of most abbreviations.

> Dr. Breslin   Mr. and Mrs. Liu   Ms. Barsky   M. A. degree

QUESTION MARK (?)

The question mark follows a direct question, as in the following examples.

> What's that green stuff in your hair?
>
> Have you seen the new Will Smith movie?
>
> "What did you put in this stew?" Grandpa asked.

Indirect questions, those that tell the reader about a question rather than ask it directly, do not require question marks. They end with periods.

> Please ask the bus driver if we can get off at Spruce Street.
>
> I wonder if I'll ever see Ali again.
>
> Gina asked Stan to jump-start her car.

EXCLAMATION POINT (!)

The exclamation point shows that a word or statement expresses excitement or another strong feeling.

> Look out for that car!
>
> I've won the lottery!
>
> If you insult my dog again, I'll let go of the leash!

Note   Exclamation points lose their power if they are used too frequently. When they are used occasionally and for good reason, they add drama to a paragraph.

Practice 1

Place a period, question mark, or exclamation point at the end of each of the following sentences.

1. When does the library close
2. Many rush-hour drivers are impatient and aggressive
3. Hurry up if you want to see the cat giving birth
4. Although I followed the directions closely, the computer program didn't run
5. Please put all cans and glass bottles in the recycling bins

COLON (:)

The colon says, in essence, "Keep reading. Here comes something important." It has three uses:

To introduce a list. The bag lady's possessions were few: a shopping cart, a sleeping bag, and two or three ragged garments.

To introduce a long or literary quotation. Charles Dickens begins his classic novel *A Tale of Two Cities* with these well-known words: "It was the best of times, it was the worst of times, it was the age of wisdom, it was the age of foolishness. . . ."

To introduce a final fact or explanation. There's only one explanation for Maude's behavior: she's jealous.

Note   Use a colon only where a period would also be appropriate.

SEMICOLON (;)

Unlike the colon, which indicates "Go on," the semicolon says "Pause here." Semicolons are used between two complete thoughts in two ways:

To join two complete thoughts not connected by a joining word. Barry cleans the house and cooks; Lana does the laundry and the grocery shopping.

To join two complete statements with a transitional word. I've never liked my father-in-law; furthermore, he knows it.

Note   Other transitional words that may come after a semicolon include *however, moreover, therefore, thus, also, consequently, otherwise, nevertheless, then, now, in addition, in fact,* and *as a result.* (A longer list appears on page 210.)

Punctuation note   Put a comma after such transitional words.

HYPHEN (-)

The hyphen is used in two ways:

To join two or more words that act together to describe a noun. We found an excuse to walk away from the fast-talking salesman. (The hyphen shows that *fast* and *talking,* combined, describe the salesman; he talks fast.)

To divide a word at the end of a line of writing. If you ever visit California, I hope you'll come see me.

Note   Always divide a word between syllables, and never divide a word of only one syllable. Your dictionary will show you where syllable divisions occur.

DASH (—)

The dash indicates a dramatic pause. By using it, the writer is giving special emphasis to the words that the dash separates from the rest of the sentence.

CPR sometimes—but not always—succeeds in reviving heart attack victims.

Randy spotted his blind date sitting in the restaurant. He straightened his tie, waved confidently to her, swaggered into the room—and tripped and fell full-length on the carpet.

Note   To type a dash, type two hyphens. Do not add space before or after a dash.

PARENTHESES ( )

Parentheses show that the information inside them is less important than the other material presented.

Professor Rodriguez (one of my favorite teachers) is going to retire this year.

The assignments that follow (Exercises 1, 2, and 3) will help sharpen your understanding of everyday defense mechanisms.

Practice 2

Insert a colon, semicolon, hyphen, a dash or dashes, or parentheses where needed in each of the sentences below. Use only one kind of mark in each sentence.

1. A black hatted man stood in the doorway.

2. My mother's college roommate I think I've mentioned her to you before has invited us to visit her in Florida.

3. As Snow White learned, apples aren't so good for you after all if they're poisoned.

4. The Swiss army knife came with many attachments a screwdriver, tweezers, magnifying glass, toothpick, and four knife blades.

5. Many people find it very hard to stay on a diet ads tempt them constantly with images of forbidden foods.

Note   Additional information about punctuation marks appears on pages 219–220.

Name _____   Section _____   Date _____

Score: (Number right) _____ × 12.5 = _____ %

■ Other Punctuation Marks: Test 1

Each of the following sentences needs one of the kinds of punctuation marks shown in the box below. In the space provided, write the letter of the mark needed. Then add that mark to the sentence. Each sentence requires a different punctuation mark.

Note   To help you master these punctuation marks, explanations are given for half of the sentences.

a	Period .	**e**	Semicolon ;
b	Question mark ?	**f**	Hyphen -
c	Exclamation point !	**g**	Dash or dashes —
d	Colon :	**h**	Parentheses ( )

_____ 1. Three languages are spoken in Switzerland German, French, and Italian.
German, French, and Italian is a list of items.

_____ 2. Which of these offices is the one that processes student loans

_____ 3. My usually soft spoken father began to shout angrily.
The words *soft* and *spoken* need to be joined into one descriptive unit.

_____ 4. Monica barely needed to study in high school however, she's finding college more difficult.

_____ 5. If you ever and I mean ever forget our anniversary again, you'd better start looking for a lawyer.
The phrase *and I mean ever* needs to be set off. It is being emphasized dramatically.

_____ 6. Paula's suede shoes the ones she'd bought in Florida were chewed up by the puppy.

_____ 7. Don't pick up that hot plate
The statement is a strong one, which would probably be shouted.

_____ 8. Warren spoke to the restaurant manager and asked if the air conditioning couldn't be turned down just a little

■ Other Punctuation Marks: Test 2

Each of the following sentences needs one of the kinds of punctuation marks shown in the box below. In the space provided, write the letter of the mark needed. Then insert the punctuation into the sentence. Each punctuation mark is used at least once.

a	Period .	**e**	Semicolon ;
b	Question mark ?	**f**	Hyphen -
c	Exclamation point !	**g**	Dash or dashes —
d	Colon :	**h**	Parentheses ( )

_____ 1. Did you know that a slow moving car can cause an accident?

_____ 2. Dozens of birds flocked around the birdfeeder a gray cat crept quietly toward them in the bushes below.

_____ 3. "DE . . . FENSE " screamed the fans as the visiting team passed the basketball back and forth.

_____ 4. I love animals however, I wouldn't want a snake as a pet.

_____ 5. The little girl looked very sad as she pulled her test out of her notebook then burst out laughing when her mother saw the A+ on it.

_____ 6. The novel *Beloved* by Toni Morrison who also wrote *The Bluest Eye* is a powerful story about the painful legacy of slavery.

_____ 7. There are two kinds of moviegoers that drive me crazy those who talk constantly and those who blurt out what is going to happen next.

_____ 8. "Hating people," wrote Harry Emerson Fosdick, "is like burning down your own house to get rid of a rat"

_____ 9. The supervisor wondered out loud, "Does Sam ever admit that he made a mistake"

_____ 10. Henry Thompson was a respected businessman, Sunday school teacher, Scout leader and occasional bank robber.

Name _____ Section _____ Date _____

■ Other Punctuation Marks: Test 3

Each of the following passages requires **two** of the punctuation marks shown in the box below. In the spaces provided, write the letters of the **two** marks needed in each passage. Then insert the correct punctuation into the sentence. Each punctuation mark is used at least once.

Note   To help you master these punctuation marks, explanations are provided for half of the corrections.

a	Period .	**e**	Semicolon ;
b	Question mark ?	**f**	Hyphen -
c	Exclamation point !	**g**	Dash or dashes —
d	Colon :	**h**	Parentheses ( )

____ ____ 1. I watched my sister searching through the drawers. Finally I asked her what she was looking for "Why do you have to know" she asked angrily.
I asked her what she was looking for is an indirect question.

____ ____ 2. Jerry's mother once worked for the Peace Corps. She traveled to several countries Thailand, India, Nepal, and Malaysia. She often told me I visited their home many times that Nepal was the most beautiful country in the world.
Thailand, India, Nepal, and Malaysia is a list of items.

____ ____ 3. The door-to-door salesman seemed like such a shy, kind person that we invited him in for coffee. It was several hours later when he was probably in the next state that we discovered he had robbed us.
The words *when he was probably in the next state* should be emphasized.

____ ____ 4. When I came downstairs, the kitchen was deserted. A single half eaten doughnut was all that remained in the box. I stared at the box I couldn't believe my eyes and shouted, "Who ate all the doughnuts?"
Half and *eaten* are acting together to describe a noun, *doughnut.*

____ ____ 5. Ron glanced out the diner window onto the parking lot then he jumped to his feet. "They're towing away my truck" he exclaimed as he ran out the door.
The word group beginning with *Ron glanced* is actually two complete thoughts that have been run together with no mark of punctuation between them.

■ Other Punctuation Marks: Test 4

Each of the following passages requires **two** of the punctuation marks shown in the box below. In the spaces provided, write the letters of the **two** marks needed in each passage. Then insert the correct punctuation into the sentence. Each punctuation mark is used at least once.

a	Period .	**e**	Semicolon ;
b	Question mark ?	**f**	Hyphen -
c	Exclamation point !	**g**	Dash or dashes —
d	Colon :	**h**	Parentheses ( )

____ ____ 1. The hard working clerks in the billing office use humorous messages to remind people to pay their bills. Their current favorite is this one "Dear Customer, You have been on our books for a year. We have carried you longer than your mother did."

____ ____ 2. I helped my brother clean the house otherwise, he never would have gotten it done in time. I swept under the radiators a job he usually forgets and dusted the furniture.

____ ____ 3. Raoul dressed carefully for his big date He wore his gray suit, new shoes, and a handsome shirt and tie. Just before he went out the door, he glanced in the mirror to admire himself and noticed he had forgotten to shave.

____ ____ 4. During the tourist season June through August the population of the seaside town nearly doubles. Tourists come to enjoy cool sea breezes, fresh caught seafood, and, best of all, splashing in the Atlantic.

____ ____ 5. "I can't stand it when people keep taking my pencils" Sandy screamed. "Don't they realize I occasionally need to write something down"

Name _____ Section _____ Date _____

Score: (Number right) _____ × 10 = _____%

■ Other Punctuation Marks: Test 5

Each of the ten sentences in the passage below requires punctuation: a colon, semicolon, hyphen, dash or dashes, or parentheses. In each sentence, underline the place where punctuation is needed. Then write the corrections on the lines provided. When you write each correction, include the words before and after the punctuation mark.

Note   To help you master these punctuation marks, directions are given for half of the corrections.

[1]Everyone has a bad dream at times moreover, people often have the same nightmare repeatedly. [2]My friend Carla I've known her since kindergarten frequently dreams she is falling off a cliff. [3]"It's always a slow motion fall," she says, adding, "I have lots of time to be terrified, but I never hit bottom." [4]My roommate Cassie's nightmare is of a huge red boulder always exactly the same size and color rolling down a hill toward her. [5]My father's dream has been the same for years a black cat is sitting on his chest, suffocating him. [6]In my most frequent nightmare, I'm trying to walk somewhere my shoes are terribly slippery. [7]I can see my destination often an exam room on campus, but I just can't get there. [8]My sense of ever increasing frustration stays with me long after I wake up. [9]Psychologists say that nightmares especially the recurring kind tell us a great deal about our inner fears. [10]My particular fear seems obvious it's the fear that I'm incapable of reaching my goals.

1. _____ Add a semicolon.

2. _____

3. _____ Add a hyphen.

4. _____

5. _____ Add a colon.

6. _____

7. _____ Add parentheses.

8. _____

9. _____ Add two dashes.

10. _____

Name _____   Section _____   Date _____

Score: (Number right) _____ × 10 = _____%

■ Other Punctuation Marks: Test 6

Each of the ten sentences in the passage below requires punctuation: a colon, semicolon, hyphen, dash or dashes, or parentheses. In each sentence, underline the place where punctuation is needed. Then write the corrections on the lines provided. When you write each correction, include the words before and after the punctuation mark.

[1]The late Theodor Seuss Geisel better known as Dr. Seuss was one of the most influential children's authors of the twentieth century. [2]Before starting to write children's books, he worked in advertising for fifteen years, drawing large, weird looking bugs in ads for an insecticide called Flit. [3]During World War II, he helped the war effort in several ways drawing political cartoons, writing and producing documentaries, and creating animated training films with rhymed scripts. [4]His first children's book was rejected by more than twenty different publishers however, Geisel continued to write. [5]Eventually he became a successful, award winning author. [6]His children's books have sold more than 200,000,000 copies and have been translated into more than 15 languages Latin and Hebrew, to name just two. [7]Geisel's work earned him a variety of awards three Academy Awards, an Emmy, a Pulitzer Prize, and three Caldecott Honor Awards for children's book illustration. [8]Some of Geisel's books specifically the later ones deal with contemporary issues. [9]*The Lorax* expresses Geisel's concern for the environment *The Butter Battle Book* shows the danger of the arms race. [10]Dr. Seuss revolutionized reading instruction by teaching a valuable lesson to both children and adults reading can be fun.

1. _____

_____

2. _____

3. _____

4. _____

5. _____

6. _____

7. _____

8. _____

9. _____

10. _____

12 Capital Letters

Seeing What You Know

Place capital letters on the words that need them in the following sentences. Then check your answers by reading the explanations below.

1. the coach growled, "if i see you drop one more pass, ed, you're off the team."

2. At bronx community college in new york, students can take night courses in hispanic literature and asian cooking as well as english.

3. Did you know that thanksgiving is always the fourth thursday in november?

4. At breakfast I often read the latest issue of *people* while eating wheaties sprinkled with raisins and toast spread with skippy peanut butter.

Understanding the Answers

1. **The** coach growled, "**If I** see you drop one more pass, **Ed,** you're off the team."
   The first word of a sentence, the first word of a quoted sentence, the pronoun *I,* and people's names are capitalized. *Coach* and *team,* which are general terms (not specific names), are not capitalized.

2. At **B**ronx **C**ommunity **C**ollege in **N**ew **Y**ork, students can take night courses in **H**ispanic literature and **A**sian cooking as well as **E**nglish.
   Capital letters are used for names of specific places. Names of races, nationalities, and languages are also capitalized. *Students, night courses, literature,* and *cooking* are general terms that are not capitalized.

3. Did you know that **T**hanksgiving is always the fourth **T**hursday in **N**ovember?
   The names of holidays, days of the week, and months are always capitalized.

4. At breakfast I often read the latest issue of ***P**eople* while eating **W**heaties sprinkled with raisins and toast spread with **S**kippy peanut butter.
   Titles of magazines and brand names of products are capitalized. General words like *raisins, toast,* and *peanut butter* are not capitalized.

Capital letters have many uses, the most common of which appear in this chapter.

THE FIRST WORD IN A SENTENCE OR DIRECT QUOTATION

Sentences begin with capital letters. The first word of a quoted sentence is also capitalized.

My sister said, "Don't forget Nick's surprise party. It's Friday at 8 P.M."

"Let's hope," I replied, "that nobody tells Nick about it."

In the second sentence, the word *that* is not capitalized because it does not start a sentence. It is part of the sentence that begins with the words *Let's hope.*

THE WORD "I" AND PEOPLE'S NAMES

"Today I got a call from an old high school friend, Dick Hess," Sandy said.

Note   A title that comes before someone's name is treated as part of the name.

Next week Uncle Dave and Aunt Gloria are seeing Dr. Mendell for checkups.

But: My uncle and aunt go to the best doctor in town.

NAMES OF SPECIFIC PLACES AND LANGUAGES

In general, if something is on a map (including a street map), capitalize it.

Frankie graduated from Kennedy High School on Main Street, left her home in Altoona, Pennsylvania, moved to New York, and took a job as a waitress in a Greenwich Village restaurant.

Note   Places that are not specifically named do not require capital letters.

Frankie graduated from high school, left her home in a small town, moved to the big city, and took a job as a waitress in a neighborhood restaurant.

The names of languages come from place names, so languages are also capitalized.

Inez, who was born in Spain, speaks fluent Spanish as well as English.

NAMES OF SPECIFIC GROUPS (RACES, RELIGIONS, NATIONALITIES, COMPANIES, CLUBS, AND OTHER ORGANIZATIONS)

Although Barbara is Lutheran and Mark is Jewish, and she is his boss at the local Home Depot store, their marriage seems to work very well.

The robbery suspect is a six-foot-tall Caucasian male with a German accent.

The American Civil Liberties Union supports the Ku Klux Klan's right to demonstrate.

Practice 1

Place capital letters on the words that need them in the sentences below.

1. as we watched the movie, doug leaned over and whispered, "don't you think this is pretty boring?"

2. st. mary's seminary in baltimore, maryland, has trained catholic priests for more than two hundred years.

3. we decided to hold the retirement dinner for professor henderson at the florentine, the new italian restaurant on lake street.

4. some of the most expensive shops in the world are found along rodeo drive in beverly hills, california.

5. "when I was a kid," the comedian rodney dangerfield told his audience, "my parents moved a lot—but i always found them."

CALENDAR ITEMS

Basically, everything on a calendar—including names of days of the week, months, and holidays—should be capitalized. The only exceptions are the names of the seasons (*spring, summer, fall, winter*), which are not capitalized.

Since Joy was born on **D**ecember 26, her family celebrates her birthday on **C**hristmas **D**ay.

Next **M**onday, which is **L**abor **D**ay, all government offices will be closed.

Stan watches baseball on television in the spring and summer, football in the fall, and basketball in the winter.

PRODUCT NAMES

Capitalize the copyrighted brand name of a product, but not the kind of product it names.

Pilar won't buy presweetened cereals for her children. She prefers less sugary brands such as **C**heerios and **W**heat **C**hex.

Our cats have refused to eat any more **F**riskies or **N**ine **L**ives cat food. They insist on eating **S**tarkist tuna—right off our plates.

TITLES

The titles of books, television or stage shows, songs, magazines, movies, articles, poems, stories, papers, and so forth are capitalized.

The book *Shoeless Joe* was made into the movie *Field of Dreams*.

I'd much rather read *Newsweek* than the *New York Times*.

Professor Martin praised Aisha's term paper, "**T**he **S**ocial **I**mpact of the **I**ndustrial **R**evolution," but he suggested that she revise one section.

Note   The words *the, of, a, an, and,* and other short, unstressed words are not capitalized when they appear in the middle of a title.

FAMILY WORDS THAT SUBSTITUTE FOR NAMES

When I was a little girl, **G**randma was my favorite baby-sitter.

I'll ask **D**ad if he'd like to go to the movie with us.

Capitalize a word such as *grandma* or *dad* only if it is being used as a substitute for that person's name. Do not capitalize words showing family relationships when they are preceded by possessive words such as *my, her,* or *our.*

Did you know that my grandmother goes to the racetrack every week?

SPECIFIC SCHOOL COURSES

Capitalize the names of specific courses, including those containing a number.

To graduate, I need to take **A**dvanced **B**iology, **S**peech 102, and **L**iterature of **O**ther **C**ultures.

But the names of general subject areas are not capitalized.

To graduate, I still need to take a biology course, a speech course, and a literature course.

Practice 2

Place capital letters on the words that need them in the sentences below.

1. Our student body is about 50 percent caucasian, 30 percent african-american, and 10 percent each hispanic and asian.

2. Elvis Presley's hit song "all shook up" was inspired by a bottle of pepsi.

3. Rashid heard that introduction to statistics was impossible to pass, so he signed up for a psychology course instead.

4. The second monday in october is celebrated as columbus day.

5. "But, mommy, it *hurts!*" the boy whimpered as his mother dabbed solarcaine lotion on his sunburn.

Note   Additional information about capital letters appears on pages 221–222.

Name _____   Section _____   Date _____

Score: (Number right) _____ × 4 = _____%

■ **Capital Letters: Test 1**

Underline the words that need to be capitalized. Then write the words correctly in the spaces provided. The number of spaces shows how many capital letters are missing in each sentence.

Note   To help you master capitalization, explanations are given for half of the sentences.

1. My uncle, dr. lopez, works at southside clinic.

   _____   _____   _____   _____

   Capitalize people's names, titles that come before names, and names of specific places.

2. A story about my disabled boss, ted, once appeared in *sports illustrated*.

   _____   _____   _____

3. when dad shouted, "don't move!" I froze in fear.

   _____   _____   _____

   Capitalize the first word of a sentence and of a direct quotation. Also capitalize a word used instead of a person's name.

4. The speaker at parkside college's graduation was senator holland.

   _____   _____   _____   _____

5. Every january, renee's grandparents travel to florida for a winter vacation.

   _____   _____   _____

   Capitalize the name of a month, of a particular person, and of a particular place.

6. When the door opened, aunt sarah whispered, "bring in the birthday cake now; then start singing."

   _____   _____   _____

7. Most british people who attend church belong to the church of england.

   _____   _____   _____

   Capitalize names of nationalities. Also capitalize names of religions. Short, unstressed words in the middle of a name are not capitalized.

8. The television show *60 minutes* is Fran's favorite; she's writing a paper about one of its stories for sociology 101.

   _____   _____

Name _____ Section _____ Date _____

Score: (Number right) _____ × 2.5 = _____ %

■ Capital Letters: Test 2

Underline the words that need to be capitalized. Then write the words correctly in the spaces provided. The number of spaces shows how many capital letters are missing in each sentence.

1. Years ago i knew a guy named andy who lived on forest avenue.

    _____   _____   _____   _____

2. The city of new orleans is famous for its celebration of the holiday mardi gras.

    _____   _____   _____   _____

3. In one of his best-remembered speeches, president john kennedy said, "ask not what your country can do for you; ask what you can do for your country."

    _____   _____   _____   _____

4. Since you're going to the supermarket, could you get me a carton of tropicana orange juice, a box of tide, and a can of maxwell house coffee?

    _____   _____   _____   _____

5. *Interview with the vampire,* a book by anne rice, is about a vampire named louis.

    _____   _____   _____   _____

6. The teenagers cruised down grant drive and then headed over to concord mall.

    _____   _____   _____   _____

7. Many years ago, people in hollywood told arnold schwarzenegger he would never succeed as an actor because of his austrian accent.

    _____   _____   _____   _____

8. I last saw grandpa and aunt rhoda at my cousin's wedding in march.

    _____   _____   _____   _____

9. The high school choir performed some african-american spirituals as well as a piece by franz schubert.

    _____   _____   _____   _____

10. A popular ad campaign for chevrolet featured the song "the heartbeat of america."

    _____   _____   _____   _____

Name _____ Section _____ Date _____

Score: (Number right) _____ × 10 = _____%

■ Capital Letters: Test 3

Underline the **two** words that require capital letters in each group of sentences below. Then write the words (with capital letters) in the spaces provided.

Note   To help you master capitalization, explanations are given for one item in each sentence.

1. I don't know my way around chicago well. If I get too far away from the downtown area known as the loop, I become hopelessly lost. All the streets look the same to me.

    a. _____   Names of specific places are capitalized.

    b. _____

2. Winter is my favorite season. However, my brother says, "what moron likes to be cold and wet all the time? Warm, beautiful june, the beginning of summer, is the best time of year."

    a. _____   Capitalize the first word of a quoted sentence.

    b. _____

3. Lillian, who is Methodist, had never visited a catholic church before. She went with her friend Henry to attend an easter service there. Afterward they stayed for a meal in the church's fellowship hall.

    a. _____   Names of religions are capitalized.

    b. _____

4. Jasmin's husband teaches an evening class once a week. Since he comes home late on wednesdays, Jasmin often takes the children out for supper on that night. This week the kids have asked to eat at Burger king.

    a. _____   Days of the week are capitalized.

    b. _____

5. My cousin is studying to be a teacher. For a course called Introduction to teaching, she was asked to read a book by Jonathan Kozol called *Savage inequalities,* which criticizes public schools. She now wants to be a public school teacher and help inner-city children get the best education possible.

    a. _____   Names of specific school courses are capitalized.

    b. _____

■ Capital Letters: Test 4

Underline the **two** words that require capital letters in each group of sentences below. Then write the words (with capital letters) in the spaces provided.

1. Karen stayed after class to talk over her grade with professor Hartzler. Although she enjoyed her french classes, she wasn't doing very well. Her professor suggested that Karen get some extra tutoring in the language.

   a. _____

   b. _____

2. Is your uncle going to come to the party? I'd like him to meet aunt Lydia. They're both single and active in the democratic party. Maybe they would like each other.

   a. _____

   b. _____

3. Although grandpa lives in New England for most of the year, he travels to a warmer climate for the winter. He says, "when the snow flies, so do I."

   a. _____

   b. _____

4. Amanda visited New mexico last summer. She was fascinated by the mix of Native American and spanish cultures there. She is reading everything she can find about this region and hopes to go back again someday.

   a. _____

   b. _____

5. Now that Betsy has small children to take along, she no longer enjoys trips to the mall. It's easier for her to buy from catalogs or online. Last week, she ordered clothing from the coldwater creek catalog and computer supplies from two different Web sites.

   a. _____

   b. _____

Name _____ Section _____ Date _____

Score: (Number right) _____ × 4 = _____%

■ ## Capital Letters: Test 5

Each sentence in the passage below contains one or more words that require capitalization. Underline these words; then write the words (with capital letters) on the lines below. The number of spaces shows how many capital letters are needed in each sentence.

Note   To help you master capitalization, explanations are given for half of the sentences.

¹last summer my husband jerry and i decided to take a vacation. ²As we discussed where we should go, I jokingly said, "you know, we never got to niagara falls on our honeymoon." ³Next thing we knew, we had a house full of road maps and literature from the niagara chamber of commerce. ⁴On the second monday in july, we hopped into our car and headed for the canadian border. ⁵It was a long drive, so we took turns driving and passed some time singing old songs like "home on the range." ⁶When jerry drove, I often read the recent issues of *time* that I'd brought along to catch up on the news. ⁷finally we arrived at our destination, a hotel full of interesting people, including lots of japanese tourists. ⁸There was also a lively convention of people belonging to the american association of retired persons. ⁹That very night, after sending picture postcards to mom and dad, we went out to get our first look at the falls in the dark. ¹⁰Although I'd grown up looking at pictures of the falls on boxes of nabisco cereals, nothing could have prepared me for the majestic beauty of the real thing.

1. _____   _____   _____
   Capitalize the first word of a sentence, people's names, and the word *I*. Names of seasons are not capitalized.

2. _____   _____   _____

3. _____   _____   _____
   Names of particular organizations are capitalized.

4. _____   _____   _____

5. _____   _____
   Capitalize song titles. Do not capitalize short, unstressed words in the middles of titles.

6. _____   _____

7. _____   _____
   Capitalize the first word of a sentence and the names of nationalities.

8. _____   _____   _____   _____

9. _____   _____
   Capitalize names of relatives used in place of their actual names. The word *falls* is used here as a general term, so it is not capitalized.

10. _____

Name _____   Section _____   Date _____

Score: (Number right) _____ × 4 = _____ %

■ Capital Letters: Test 6

Each sentence in the passage below contains one or more words that require capitalization. Underline these words; then write the words (with capital letters) on the lines below. The number of spaces shows how many capital letters are needed in each sentence.

¹Perhaps you have heard of the book, play, or movie called *meet me in st. louis.* ²The story is set in 1904 during a fair officially called the louisiana purchase exposition. ³This fair was huge, spanning more than 1200 acres and including much of forest park and washington university. ⁴In addition to states and territories of the united states, more than fifty foreign countries participated in the fair. ⁵For their headquarters, many states and countries built structures that duplicated important buildings; for example, virginia's pavilion was a replica of thomas jefferson's home. ⁶Visitors to the fair saw things they had never seen before—automobiles, airplanes, motion pictures, buildings lit by electricity, entire villages of natives from the philippine islands. ⁷The fair's emphasis was on processes; at an exhibit sponsored by the brown shoe company, for instance, people could see shoes being made. ⁸More than 20,000,000 people visited the fair between april 30 and december 1. ⁹Even the olympics—the first ones to award medals—were part of this remarkable fair. ¹⁰souvenirs and memorabilia from this fair are now scattered throughout the world.

1. _____   _____   _____   _____
2. _____   _____   _____
3. _____   _____   _____   _____
4. _____   _____
5. _____   _____   _____
6. _____   _____
7. _____   _____   _____
8. _____   _____
9. _____
10. _____

13 Homonyms

Seeing What You Know

In the following sentences, underline each correct word in parentheses. Then read the explanations below.

1. (You're, Your) the only student (who's, whose) always (hear, here) on time.

2. (Its, It's) difficult to (break, brake) the habit of smoking.

3. I never (knew, new) that (there, they're) could be such a problem as having (too, to) little money to get through the month.

4. The Fergusons found that (their, there) dog had eaten the (hole, whole) ham.

5. The (plane, plain) had (two, too) engines, and one of them caught on fire.

Understanding the Answers

1. **You're** the only student **who's** always **here** on time.
   You're is the contraction of the words *you* and *are*. *Who's* is the contraction of the words *who is*. *Here* means "in this place."

2. **It's** difficult to **break** the habit of smoking.
   It's is the contraction of the words *it* and *is*. *Break* means "end."

3. I never **knew** that **there** could be such a problem as having **too** little money to get through the month.
   Knew is the past tense of *know*. *There* is used with forms of the verb *to be—is, are, was, were,* and so on. *Too* means "extremely."

4. The Fergusons found that **their** dog had eaten the **whole** ham.
   Their means "belonging to them." *Whole* means "entire."

5. The **plane** had **two** engines, and one of them caught on fire.
   Plane means "airplane." *Two* is the spelling of the number 2.

This chapter looks at a number of words that are mistaken for one another because they are **homonyms**: words that are pronounced the same (or almost the same) but are spelled differently and are different in meaning.

THE BIG FOUR

Of all frequently confused homonyms, the following four groups cause writers the most trouble:

its   *belonging to it*
it's   contraction of *it is*

If the house doesn't get **its** roof repaired soon, **it's** going to be full of water. (If the house doesn't get the roof *belonging to it* repaired, *it is* going to be full of water.)

It's a shame that the new restaurant lost **its** license. (*It is* a shame that the new restaurant lost the license *belonging to it.*)

their   *belonging to them*
there   (1) *in that place;* (2) used with *is, are, was, were,* and other forms of the verb *to be*
they're contraction of *they are*

The coach told the players that **there** was no excuse for **their** unprofessional behavior; **they're** going to run extra laps as punishment. (The coach told the players *there was* [form of *to be*] no excuse for the unprofessional behavior *belonging to them; they are* going to run extra laps as punishment.)

They're showing all the *Star Trek* movies in order at **their** science fiction convention; I'm going to get **there** early. (*They are* showing all the *Star Trek* movies in order at the science fiction convention *belonging to them;* I'm going to get *to that place* early.)

to   (1) used before a verb, as in *to say;* (2) *toward*
too   (1) *overly* or *extremely;* (2) *also*
two   *the number 2*

It would be **too** confusing **to** name the baby Lucy; her mother and **two** of her cousins are named Lucy **too**. (It would be *overly* confusing *to name* [verb] the baby Lucy; her mother and *2* of her cousins are named Lucy *also.*)

Let's go **to** the mall **to** look for clothes, unless you are **too** tired. (Let's go *toward* the mall *to look* [verb] for clothes, unless you are *overly* tired.)

your   *belonging to you*
you're   contraction of *you are*

If **you're** going out in this downpour, take **your** umbrella. (If *you are* going out in this downpour, take the umbrella *belonging to you.*)

Do you think **your** family will be upset when they learn **you're** moving to Alaska? (Do you think the family *belonging to you* will be upset when they learn *you are* moving to Alaska?)

Practice

Underline the correct homonym in each group.

1. (Its, It's) a shame (its, it's) going to rain today; we won't be able to give the front porch (its, it's) second coat of paint.

2. (Their, There, They're) isn't any good reason to give the twins (their, there, they're) birthday presents early; (their, there, they're) just going to want more presents when the real birthday comes around.

3. Having (to, too, two) read and take notes on (to, too, two) chapters a night is simply (to, too, two) much work.

4. (Your, You're) not serious when you say (your, you're) planning to sell (your, you're) house and live in a tent in the woods, are you?

OTHER COMMON HOMONYMS

brake   (1) *to slow* or *to stop;* (2) *mechanism that stops a moving vehicle*
break   (1) *to cause to come apart;* (2) *to bring to an end*

If you don't **brake** your sled as you go down the icy hill, you could easily **break** a leg.

hear   (1) *to take in by ear;* (2) *to be informed*
here   *in this place*

The music **here** near the band is so loud that I can't **hear** you.

hole   *empty or hollow spot*
whole   *complete* or *entire*

The mechanic examined the **whole** surface of the flat tire before finding a tiny **hole** near the rim.

knew   (past tense of *know*) (1) *understood;* (2) *was or were aware of*
new   (1) *not old;* (2) *recently arrived*

Jay **knew** he needed a **new** bike when his old one broke down again yesterday.

know   (1) *to understand;* (2) *to be aware of*
no   (1) *not any;* (2) *opposite of yes*

I have **no** idea how much other people **know** about my divorce.

passed   (past tense of *pass*) (1) *handed to;* (2) *went by;* (3) *completed successfully*
past   (1) *time before the present;* (2) *by*

As Ben walked **past** Sharon's desk, he **passed** her a Valentine and pleaded, "Let's forget about the **past** and be friends again."

peace   *calmness* or *quiet*
piece   *portion of something*

The usual **peace** of the house was disturbed when my brother discovered that someone had eaten a **piece** of the cake he had baked for his girlfriend's birthday.

plain   (1) *not fancy;* (2) *obvious;* (3) *straightforward*
plane   shortened form of *airplane*

It was **plain** to see that a **plane** had recently landed in the muddy field.

right   (1) *correct;* (2) *opposite of left*
write   *to form letters and words*

I can **write** clearly using my **right** hand; when I use my left, my writing is illegible.

than   word used in comparisons
then   (1) *at that time;* (2) *next;* (3) *as a consequence* (with *if*)

First Aaron realized he was driving faster **than** the speed limit; **then** he saw the police car behind him.

threw   (past tense of *throw*) *tossed*
through   (1) *into and out of;* (2) *finished*

Yesterday I went **through** my old letters and **threw** most of them away.

wear   *to put on* (as with clothing)
where   *in what place* or *to what place*

Because Samantha was not told **where** her friends were taking her for her birthday, she had trouble deciding what to **wear**.

weather   *outside conditions* (rain, wind, temperature, etc.)
whether   *if*

The **weather** won't spoil my vacation; **whether** it rains or not, my days will be spent on the beach.

who's   contraction of *who is* or *who has*
whose   *belonging to whom*

The boss yelled, "**Who's** responsible for this mistake? **Whose** fault is it?"

> Note   Additional information about homonyms and other confusing words appears on pages 223–225.

Name _____ Section _____ Date _____

■ Homonyms: Test 1

In the ten sentences below, underline the correct word in each group of homonyms.

Note   To help you review some of the homonyms in this chapter, use the definitions given in half of the sentences.

1. Did you (here, hear) the old legend about a famous Native American chief who is buried (here, hear)?
    Did you take in by ear *the old legend about a famous Native American chief who is buried* in this place*?*

2. (To, Too) many people wanted tickets for the concert, so the promoters decided (to, too) add a second concert the following night.

3. The stray dog can't make up (it's, its) mind whether to trust me or not, so (it's, its) still sitting in the driveway watching me.
    The stray dog can't make up the mind belonging to it *whether to trust me or not, so* it is *still sitting in the driveway watching me.*

4. Some customers don't (no, know) how to say (no, know) to salespeople.

5. (Their, There, They're) too afraid of spiders to appreciate (their, there, they're) remarkable beauty.
    They are too afraid of spiders to appreciate the remarkable beauty *belonging to them.*

6. My young niece is crying because she just (threw, through) her soccer ball (threw, through) our neighbors' kitchen window.

7. The loud whistling call of a blue jay about to feed on a (peace, piece) of bread was the only sound to be heard amid the (peace, piece) and quiet.
    The loud whistling call of a blue jay about to feed on a portion *of bread was the only sound to be heard amid the* calmness *and quiet.*

8. Pointing to the chunk of cheese on the table, the little boy said, "Couldn't you afford cheese that was (hole, whole)?" He didn't know that Swiss cheese always has (holes, wholes) in it.

9. The (knew, new) student in Spanish class (knew, new) how to speak the language better than anyone else.
    The recently arrived *student in Spanish class* understood *how to speak the language better than anyone else.*

10. (Your, You're) not supposed to dial 911 unless, in (your, you're) opinion, there's a life-threatening emergency.

■ Homonyms: Test 2

Underline the correct word in each group of homonyms.

1. I know you are angry about seeing me at Elaine's house, but (their, there, they're) was a good reason for me to go (their, there, they're).

2. If you don't (brake, break) before you go over the speed bump, you're going to (brake, break) the shock absorbers.

3. A large paperback bookstore is opening right (hear, here) on campus, and I (hear, here) it plans to sell computer supplies as well as books.

4. Since you (knew, new) that Suki's car was (knew, new), you should have been especially careful with it.

5. (Its, It's) easy to see from your face that your day has had (its, it's) bad moments.

6. On the celebrity tour, we drove (passed, past) several movie stars' homes; we also (passed, past) the restaurant where many Hollywood people have lunch.

7. The two brothers have not had any (peace, piece) ever since they began arguing over a small (peace, piece) of property their father left them.

8. (Whose, Who's) shoes are these in the middle of the floor, and (whose, who's) been messy enough to leave crumbs all over the table?

9. The teacher told Richard to (right, write) the assignment on the (right, write) side of the blackboard.

10. (Wear, Where) in this store might I find something appropriate to (wear, where) to a job interview?

Name _____ Section _____ Date _____

Score: (Number right) _____ × 10 = _____ %

■ Homonyms: Test 3

Each short paragraph below contains **two** homonym errors. Find these errors and underline them. Then write the correct words in the spaces provided.

Note   To help you review some of the homonyms in this chapter, use the hints given for half of the homonyms.

1. If its sunny tomorrow, our English class will meet outside. Unfortunately, we can't know in advance what the whether will be. Even if we meet inside, though, our teacher has promised us an unusual class.

   a. _____   If *it is* sunny tomorrow

   b. _____

2. It's important to provide an adequate and safe supply of drinking water. Not having enough water to drink is more dangerous then having to little food. Humans will die of thirst long before they die of hunger.

   a. _____   Not having water to drink is *being*

   b. _____   *compared with* not having food to eat.

3. There are to many interesting courses being offered this year. It's difficult to choose which ones to take. Should I sign up for something I enjoy, like psychology, or should I take computer science and try to learn a new skill? Their both good choices.

   a. _____   *Overly* many courses

   b. _____

4. After experiencing a tragedy in her life, my aunt began to talk to a counselor. "I can't change the passed," she said, "but it's plane to me that talking can help me cope with it better."

   a. _____   She can't change what happened in

   b. _____   the *time before the present.*

5. Most people no the swastika as a symbol of Nazi Germany. However, the swastika, or "hooked cross," existed long before Hitler came to power. Ancient Norsemen and Native Americans new it as a symbol of the sun's journey through the sky.

   a. _____   Most people *are aware of* the swastika.

   b. _____

■ Homonyms: Test 4

Each short paragraph below contains **two** homonym errors. Find these errors and underline them. Then write the correct words in the spaces provided.

1. Because my family is so large, the hole family rarely drives anywhere together. Usually four of the children will drive with one parent and five with the other. There are always arguments among the youngest children about who's turn it is to ride in the front seats.

   a. _____

   b. _____

2. The doctor spoke sternly to Donald at his last checkup. "Your overweight, and you almost never exercise," the doctor warned. "I'm telling you in plane language that you're asking for a heart attack."

   a. _____

   b. _____

3. Some parents try to limit the amount of television their children watch. They believe that more then an hour a day of television interferes with schoolwork. They also don't like much of the language that kids here on TV shows.

   a. _____

   b. _____

4. Medical researchers have found that if your often in a bad mood, its more likely you will die of a stress-related disease such as high blood pressure, heart disease, or stroke. To live longer, they advise, take the steps needed to achieve inner peace.

   a. _____

   b. _____

5. The legend of the vampire Dracula is based on the story of a real-life Romanian prince named Vlad, who lived more than five hundred years ago. Vlad was a bloodthirsty madman who may have killed as many as 100,000 people during his six years in power. His favorite method of killing was two run a stake threw his victims. Vlad was finally killed in 1476.

   a. _____

   b. _____

Name _____ Section _____ Date _____

■ **Homonyms: Test 5**

Underline the correct homonym in each of the following sentences. Then, in the spaces provided, write an explanation for the answer you chose.

Note   To help you review some of the homonyms in this chapter, use the hints given for half of the homonyms.

[1]Selecting your career is one of the most important decisions you will make in your (hole, whole) life. [2]You are likely to spend more than 80,000 hours working at (your, you're) job. [3]Having an occupation that is well suited to you can help to make your working hours fulfilling rather (than, then) frustrating. [4]But how do you (know, no) which career to pursue? [5]Answering (to, too, two) questions can help you identify your expertise and your ambition. [6]First, what activities have been a source of satisfaction for you (threw, through) your life? [7]If, for example, you have enjoyed building things in the (passed, past), you are likely to enjoy a career in construction or architecture. [8]Second, what would you attempt if you (knew, new) you could not fail at it? [9]What you really *want* to do becomes (plane, plain) when you answer this question. [10]If you can realistically say that you would be able to earn a living doing an activity you love, you have probably identified a career that would be (right, write) for you.

1. _____ The sentence is talking about your *entire* life.

2. _____

3. _____ Working hours that are fulfilling are *being compared with* those that are frustrating.

4. _____

5. _____ "First" and "Second" indicate that *2* questions are being asked.

6. _____

7. _____ The sentence refers to an *earlier* time in your life.

8. _____

9. _____ What you want becomes *obvious* when you answer the question.

10. _____

Name _____   Section _____   Date _____

Score: (Number right) _____ × 10 = _____ %

■ Homonyms: Test 6

Underline the correct homonym in each of the following sentences. Then, in the spaces provided, write an explanation for the answer you chose.

[1]"(Who's, Whose) résumé is this?" asked the career counselor. [2]Jamila raised her hand, wondering (weather, whether) the counselor thought her résumé was especially good or especially bad. [3]"Let's go (threw, through) this with the class as we discuss what makes a résumé work," said the counselor.

[4]"The biggest problem is that Jamila's entries are (to, too, two) brief," he said. [5]"(Hear, Here), for instance, it says she was a secretary for three years. [6]Surely that doesn't tell the (hole, whole) story of what she did on the job. [7]I'd like to see Jamila (right, write) down every responsibility she had. [8]If she wrote her boss's letters, used a computer, supervised another employee, or planned business meetings, her résumé should let us (know, no) that. [9]Remember this: Employers only glance at most résumés as they decide if an applicant is the best person for (their, there, they're) position. [10](Your, You're) résumé must quickly provide specific information about what you are qualified to do."

1. _____

2. _____

3. _____

4. _____

5. _____

6. _____

7. _____

8. _____

9. _____

10. _____

14 Word Choice

Seeing What You Know

Imagine that the following sentences appeared in a business or school report. Check the sentence in each pair that is worded more appropriately. Then read the explanations below.

1. ____ At this point in time we have not yet scheduled the date of the exam.

   ____ We have not yet scheduled the exam.

2. ____ Fred wishes the office manager would get off his case.

   ____ Fred wishes the office manager would stop criticizing him.

3. ____ The first-grade children have been busy as bees all day, but they still seem fresh as daisies.

   ____ The first-grade children have been active all day, but they still seem energetic.

Understanding the Answers

1. **The second sentence is more direct.**
   The first sentence is longer than necessary because of the wordy expressions *at this point in time* and *scheduled the date.*

2. **The second sentence is more businesslike.**
   The slang expression *get off his case* in the first sentence is too informal for school or business writing.

3. **The second sentence is less stale.**
   The first sentence is weakened by the clichés *busy as bees* and *fresh as daisies.*

Not all writing problems involve grammar. A sentence may be grammatically correct yet fail to communicate effectively because of the words that the writer has chosen. Wordiness, slang, and clichés are three enemies of effective communication.

WORDINESS

Which of these signs would help the campus cafeteria run more smoothly?

_____ Due to the fact that our plates and our silverware are in short supply, the management kindly requests all patrons of this cafeteria, when they have finished their meals, to place all used plates and silverware on a cart before leaving the cafeteria so that they may be washed.

_____ Please put your used plates and silverware on a cart.

Wordy writing is writing that—like the first sign above—uses more words than necessary to get a message across. Such writing both confuses and irritates the reader, who resents having to wade through extra words.

To avoid wordiness, edit your writing carefully. Remove words that have the same meaning as other words in the sentence.

Wordy: In my opinion, I think that job quotas in the workplace are unfair.

Revised: I think that job quotas are unfair.

In general, work to express your thoughts in the fewest words possible that are still complete and clear. Notice, for example, how easily the following wordy expressions can be replaced by single words:

Wordy Expression	Single Word
a large number of	many
at this point in time	now
came into the possession of	obtained
despite the fact that	although
due to the fact that	because
during the time that	while
each and every day	daily
few in number	few
in order to	to
in the event that	if
in the near future	soon
in this day and age	now
is of the opinion that	believes
made the decision to	decided
on account of	because
postponed until later	postponed
small in size	small

Practice 1

Cross out the wordy expressions and unnecessary words in the sentences that follow. Then rewrite each sentence as clearly and concisely as possible.

1. Due to the fact that the judge's hair is prematurely gray at an earlier age than most women, people think she is much older than her thirty-eight years of age.

_____

_____

2. At this point in time, the company is taking a large number of steps to reduce actions that pollute the environment that is all around us.

_____

_____

3. In the event of weather that is problematic, officials will make the decision to postpone the baseball game until a later point in time.

_____

_____

SLANG

Which of the following would be appropriate to print in a newspaper?

____ The police just captured a local criminal who posed as a utility serviceman and stole from several trusting senior citizens.

____ The police just busted a local criminal who posed as a utility serviceman and ripped off several trusting senior citizens.

Slang expressions (like *busted* and *ripped off*) are part of our everyday language. They are lively and fun to use. But while slang may be appropriate in casual conversation, it generally does not belong in formal writing. Slang, by nature, is informal.

Even in less formal writing, slang is often inappropriate because not all readers understand it. Slang is frequently used by limited social groups, and it changes rapidly. When we read slang expressions from the 1960s like *groovy* or *far out,* they sound out-of-date or meaningless. Your use of slang might have the same effect on someone older (or younger) than you. For example, when you write about someone who seems confused or not very bright, "The lights are on, but nobody's home," you may know exactly what you mean. Your reader may not.

Use slang only when you have a specific purpose in mind, such as being humorous or communicating the flavor of an informal conversation.

Practice 2

Rewrite the two slang expressions (printed in *italics*) in each sentence.

1. If you want to *ace* your courses, don't *ditch* too many classes.

   _____

2. I really *lucked out.* Five people in the office were *canned,* but I kept my job.

   _____

3. Jesse finally *crashed* after *pulling an all-nighter* to finish his report.

   _____

CLICHÉS

Which of the following belongs in a nurse's daily report?

_____ The patient in 201 slept like a log until the crack of dawn.

_____ The patient in 201 slept deeply until 6:30 A.M.

A **cliché** is a commonplace, boring expression. Once, it might have been fresh, vivid, even funny. But too many people used it, so it has become stale. Don't be lazy and use other people's worn-out sayings. Find original ways to say what you mean.

Here are just a few of the many other clichés to avoid in your writing:

avoid like the plague	drive like a maniac	old as the hills
better late than never	easier said than done	pretty as a picture
busy as a bee	few and far between	scared to death
clear as a bell	in the nick of time	short and sweet
cold as ice	it goes without saying	sigh of relief
couldn't care less	last but not least	start from scratch
crazy like a fox	light as a feather	tried and true
dog-tired	needless to say	without a doubt

Practice 3

Rewrite the two clichés (printed in *italics*) in each sentence.

1. Hiroshi was *as sick as a dog* yesterday, but he looks *fit as a fiddle* today.

   _____

2. Since *time was of the essence*, I decided to *bite the bullet* and find a tutor to help me with my paper.

   _____

3. The news of the president's resignation, which came *like a bolt from the blue,* *spread like wildfire* across campus.

   _____

Note   Additional information about word choice appears on pages 226–227.

Name _____ Section _____ Date _____

Score: (Number right) _____ × 12.5 = _____%

■ Word Choice: Test 1

Each sentence below contains one or two examples of ineffective word choice. Underline each error. Then, in the space provided, write *W, S,* or *C* to indicate wordiness, slang, or cliché. Finally, use the answer line to rewrite each faulty expression, using more effective language.

Note   To help you develop skill in choosing words effectively, suggestions are given for half of the corrections.

_____   1. I was psyched to learn that classes were canceled because of the storm.

   _____

   Correct the slang.

_____   2. Most of the critics trashed the new Will Smith film.

   _____

_____   3. Due to the fact that it rained, the game was postponed until later.

   _____

   Correct the two cases of wordiness.

_____   4. Some students were late to class on account of their bus was delayed.

   _____

_____   5. The course was supposed to be hard, but it was easy as pie.

   _____

   Correct the cliché.

_____   6. The explosion made enough noise to wake the dead.

   _____

_____   7. In my opinion, I don't think there is any excuse for world hunger at this point in time.

   _____

   Correct the two cases of wordiness.

_____   8. Over fifty invitations were sent out in the mail, but only a total of twelve people responded.

   _____

Name _____   Section _____   Date _____

Score: (Number right) _____ × 10 = _____ %

■ Word Choice: Test 2

Each sentence below contains one or more examples of ineffective word choice. Underline each error. Then, in the space provided, write *W, S,* or *C* to indicate wordiness, slang, or cliché. Finally, use the answer line to rewrite each faulty expression, using more effective language.

_____   1. The job applicant wore a suit that had seen better days.

_____

_____   2. The horror movie was too gross for me.

_____

_____   3. In the event that I'm not back by three o'clock, would you put the roast in the oven?

_____

_____   4. The actor gave a shout-out to his family when he won the Academy Award.

_____

_____   5. The contestants on *American Idol* were forced to sweat it out while the judges made their decision.

_____

_____   6. The new client has not called at this point in time but is expected to do so in the very near future.

_____

_____   7. When the computer screen went blank as I was writing my report, I realized I would have to start from scratch.

_____

_____   8. The whole class freaked out when the teacher announced a surprise test.

_____

_____   9. Owing to the fact of the teachers' strike, school has not yet opened.

_____

_____   10. Velma said her boyfriend treated her like dirt, so she told him to take a hike.

_____

Name _____   Section _____   Date _____

Score: (Number right) _____ × 10 = _____%

■ Word Choice: Test 3

Each sentence below contains **two** examples of ineffective word choice. Underline each error. Then, in the space provided, write *W, S,* or *C* to indicate wordiness, slang, or cliché. Finally, use the answer line to rewrite each faulty expression, using more effective language.

Note   To help you develop skill in choosing words effectively, suggestions are given for the first correction in each group.

1. I was pleased as punch when I learned someone would be working with me today. Being in the shop alone would have been a bummer.

   ____ a. _____   Correct the cliché.

   ____ b. _____

2. It's too bad that dress is too large in size for Jen. The style and color both suit her to a T. I wonder if it could be taken in to fit her better.

   ____ a. _____   Correct the wordiness.

   ____ b. _____

3. There's never a dull moment in the Doyles' house! Yesterday the children emptied the sand that was in their sandbox onto the lawn, poured shampoo into the fish tank, and fed chocolate cake to the dog.

   ____ a. _____   Correct the cliché.

   ____ b. _____

4. Although Sheila's friends warned her that Mark was just a player, she didn't listen to them. She was head over heels about Mark. When he suddenly had no time for her, Sheila realized her friends were right.

   ____ a. _____   Correct the slang.

   ____ b. _____

5. Tired to the bone, the couple returned home after a long day's work. They were especially ticked to find a sink full of dirty dishes left by their children.

   ____ a. _____   Correct the cliché.

   ____ b. _____

■ Word Choice: Test 4

Each sentence below contains **two** examples of ineffective word choice. Underline each error. Then, in the space provided, write *W, S,* or *C* to indicate wordiness, slang, or cliché. Finally, use the answer line to rewrite each faulty expression, using more effective language.

1. Tyrell is messing with you when he says he can't be at your party. Don't listen to his teasing—he wouldn't miss that party for the world.

   _____ a. _____

   _____ b. _____

2. The last election proved that voters are sick and tired of politicians who aren't being real with them about the challenges facing the country.

   _____ a. _____

   _____ b. _____

3. Our city was hyped up even before the World Series started. Local fans were excited due to the fact that it was our team's first appearance in the World Series in 28 years.

   _____ a. _____

   _____ b. _____

4. Watching the news these days can be a real downer. Fortunately, a large number of news shows are including human-interest stories about ordinary people who are helping each other.

   _____ a. _____

   _____ b. _____

5. My uncle has been down on his luck lately. His situation took a turn for the worse when he got sick and then lost his apartment.

   _____ a. _____

   _____ b. _____

Name _____   Section _____   Date _____

Score: (Number right) _____ × 10 = _____ %

■ Word Choice: Test 5

Each sentence in the following passage contains an example of wordiness, slang, or a cliché. Underline each error. Then, in the space provided, write *W, S,* or *C* to indicate wordiness, slang, or cliché. Finally, use the answer line to rewrite the faulty expression, using more effective language.

Note   To help you develop skill in choosing words effectively, suggestions are given for half of the corrections.

[1]My sister, Elaine, never had good luck with her boyfriends, even though she's dated some hotties. [2]She always broke up with them on account of the fact that all they cared about was their gorgeous selves. [3]Then it dawned on her that she might get along better with very studious types. [4]So she started going out with nerds. [5]But she would return back home again from those dates complaining that the smart ones weren't much fun. [6]I hated to see my sister in the dumps. [7]I kept saying, "Don't lose hope—someday you'll find someone as awesome as Jeff." [8]Jeff, my boyfriend, was good-looking, did well in school, and was as sweet as pie, too. [9]During the time that Elaine was having boyfriend problems, Jeff and I often discussed her. [10]Maybe I mentioned Jeff and Elaine to each other too often; anyway, they're getting hitched this June.

1. ____ _____   Correct the slang.

2. ____ _____

3. ____ _____   Correct the cliché.

4. ____ _____

5. ____ _____   Correct the wordiness.

6. ____ _____

7. ____ _____   Correct the slang.

8. ____ _____

9. ____ _____   Correct the wordiness.

10. ____ _____

■ Word Choice: Test 6

Each sentence in the following passage contains an example of wordiness, slang, or a cliché. Underline each error. Then, in the space provided, write *W, S,* or *C* to indicate wordiness, slang, or cliché. Finally, use the answer line to rewrite the faulty expression, using more effective language.

[1]Chocolate is one of the most awesome foods in the world. [2]People began consuming unsweetened chocolate as a beverage around three thousand years ago in time in the area that is now Mexico. [3]They thought it was to die for. [4]Explorer Hernando Cortez introduced chocolate to Spain in the early 1500s, but the Spanish kept the delicacy under wraps for nearly one hundred years. [5]Once revealed, chocolate spread like wildfire across Europe. [6]By that point in time, sugar was added to the chocolate beverage; however, chocolate candy was not invented until the nineteenth century. [7]In this day and age, chocolate is a main ingredient in many snacks and desserts. [8]A serving of chocolate can provide a shot in the arm. [9]Recent research has shown that dark chocolate can strengthen the ticker and also can prevent cancer. [10]Some scientists say, however, that consuming the amount of chocolate necessary for those benefits would be like cutting off your nose to spite your face.

1. ____ _____

2. ____ _____

3. ____ _____

4. ____ _____

5. ____ _____

6. ____ _____

7. ____ _____

8. ____ _____

9. ____ _____

10. ____ _____

15 Misplaced and Dangling Modifiers

Seeing What You Know

What do you think the writer was trying to say in each of the following sentences? Underline the part of each sentence that does not seem clear. Then read the explanations below.

1. We looked at twenty-five sofas shopping on Saturday.

2. Thrown in a heap on the closet floor, Jean found her son's dirty laundry.

3. Carrying in the main course, the roast slid off its platter.

4. While taking notes in class, Jerome's thoughts were elsewhere.

Understanding the Answers

1. *Twenty-five sofas shopping on Saturday* is the unclear part of the sentence. The intended meaning is that we saw twenty-five sofas while *we* (not the twenty-five sofas) were shopping on Saturday. A better way to say so would be *Shopping on Saturday,* we looked at twenty-five sofas.

2. *Thrown in a heap on the closet floor, Jean* is the unclear part of the sentence.
   It sounds as if *Jean* was thrown on the closet floor when she found her son's laundry. The writer means, however, that Jean found *her son's dirty laundry* thrown in a heap on the closet floor.

3. *Carrying in the main course, the roast* is the unclear part of the sentence.
   The sentence seems to say that the *roast* was carrying in the main course. Actually, the roast *was* the main course; a person (not the roast) was carrying it. To make the intended meaning clear, rewrite the sentence to show who that person was: *As Stacy was* carrying in the main course, the roast slid off its platter.

4. *While taking notes in class, Jerome's thoughts* is the unclear part of the sentence.
   It sounds as if *Jerome's thoughts* were taking notes in class. The sentence needs to be rewritten like this: While *Jerome was* taking notes in class, *his* thoughts were elsewhere.

A **modifier** is one or more words that describe other words. Two common errors involving these descriptive words are misplaced modifiers and dangling modifiers.

MISPLACED MODIFIERS

When a modifier is in the wrong place, the reader may not know just what it is meant to describe. Misplaced modifiers can lead to misunderstandings—some of which are unintentionally humorous.

To correct a misplaced modifier, place it as close as possible to what it is describing, so that its meaning will be clearly understood.

Misplaced modifier: The Bensons watched the parade of high school bands sitting in chairs on their lawn.
(It sounds as if *the high school bands* were sitting in chairs, rather than the Bensons.)

Corrected version: **Sitting in chairs on their lawn, the Bensons** watched the parade of high school bands.

Misplaced modifier: Please take this book to Mrs. Bey's house which she lent to me.
(Did Mrs. Bey lend her *house* to the speaker?)

Corrected version: Please take **this book, which Mrs. Bey lent to me,** to her house.

Misplaced modifier: The holdup man ran into the bank carrying a gun.
(The *bank* was carrying a gun?)

Corrected version: **The holdup man, carrying a gun,** ran into the bank.

Practice 1

Underline the misplaced modifier in each sentence. Then rewrite the sentence, placing the modifier where it needs to go to make the meaning clear.

1. The young man gave his driver's license to the officer with shaking hands.

   _____

2. We were surprised to hear a siren driving down the country road.

   _____

3. Gina got badly sunburned after spending a day at the beach on her face and back.

   _____

4. The registrar will post the schedule for final exams on the Web site.

   _____

5. Stan bought a sports car from a fast-talking salesman with wire wheels.

   _____

SINGLE-WORD MODIFIERS

Pay special attention to single-word modifiers, such as *almost, only, nearly, hardly,* and *even.* For their meaning to be correctly understood, they should be placed directly in front of the word they describe.

Misplaced modifier: Sean won the pole vault event when he almost jumped sixteen feet.
(Did Sean think about jumping sixteen feet, but then not jump at all?)

Corrected version: Sean won the pole vault event when he **jumped almost sixteen feet**.
(The intended meaning—that Sean's winning jump was not quite sixteen feet—is now clear.)

Misplaced modifier: Tanya nearly earned a thousand dollars last summer.
(Tanya had the chance to make a lot of money but didn't take advantage of it?)

Corrected version: Tanya **earned nearly a thousand dollars** last summer.
(Now we see—she earned close to a thousand dollars.)

Practice 2

Underline the misplaced single-word modifier in each sentence. Then rewrite the sentence, placing the modifier where it will make the meaning clear.

1. I only studied for ten minutes; then I took a nap.

   _____

2. Carlos must have almost answered a hundred ads before he found a job.

   _____

3. My sister nearly spends all evening on the telephone.

   _____

DANGLING MODIFIERS

A modifier that starts a sentence must be followed right away by the word it is meant to describe. Otherwise, the modifier is said to be dangling, and the sentence takes on an unintended meaning. Look at this example:

Staring dreamily off into space, the teacher's loud voice startled me.

The modifier *staring dreamily off into space* is followed by *the teacher's loud voice,* giving the impression that the voice was staring off into space. However, this is not what the author intended. The modifier was meant to describe a word that is missing: *I.*

There are two ways to correct a dangling modifier:

1   Add a subject and verb to the opening word group, and revise as necessary.

    As I was staring dreamily off into space, the teacher's loud voice startled me.

2   Place the word or words being described immediately after the opening word group, and revise as necessary.

    Staring dreamily off into space, **I was startled by** the teacher's loud voice.

Here are more examples of dangling modifiers and ways they can be corrected:

Dangling modifier: When pulling out of the driveway, the hedge blocks Tracy's view.
(Is the *hedge* pulling out of the driveway?)

Corrected versions: **Whenever Tracy pulls** out of the driveway, the hedge blocks **her** view. *Or:* When pulling out of the driveway, **Tracy finds that** the hedge blocks **her** view.

Dangling modifier: Delighted with the movie, conversation over coffee ended our evening.
(Was the *conversation* delighted with the movie?)

Corrected versions: **We were** delighted with the movie **and** ended our evening **with** conversation over coffee. *Or:* Delighted with the movie, **we** ended our evening **with** conversation over coffee.

Practice 3

In each sentence, underline the dangling modifier. Then, on the line provided, rewrite the sentence so that the intended meaning is clear. Use both methods of fixing dangling modifiers.

1. While taking a shower, a mouse ran across my bathroom floor.

    _____

2. Sitting on the front porch, mosquitoes became annoying.

    _____

3. While eating at the restaurant, Kareem's coat was stolen.

    _____

4. Breathing heavily, the finish line finally came into the runner's view.

    _____

5. Hoping to catch a glimpse of the band, the parking lot was full of fans.

    _____

Name _____ Section _____ Date _____

Score: (Number right) _____ × 12.5 = _____%

■ Misplaced and Dangling Modifiers: Test 1

In each sentence, underline the one misplaced or dangling modifier. (The first four sentences contain misplaced modifiers; the second four sentences contain dangling modifiers.) Then rewrite each sentence so that its intended meaning is clear.

Note   To help you correct misplaced and dangling modifiers, explanations are given for half of the sentences.

1. Kwan returned the overdue book to the librarian behind the desk with apologies.

_____

The sentence suggests that the desk had apologies. The modifier *with apologies* needs to be placed next to *Kwan.*

2. A group of students talked about fishing with live bait in shop class.

_____

3. The shipwrecked sailors almost went without food and water for a week.

_____

The sentence suggests that the sailors were in danger of going without food and water but avoided this danger. The writer actually means that the sailors *did* go without food and water—for just under a week.

4. Invitations to graduation exercises were nearly sent out to five hundred people.

_____

5. Jumping at a sudden noise, the razor nicked Dean's face.

_____

Dean, not the razor, was the one who jumped at a sudden noise.

6. Just before leaving for home, the secretary's telephone rang.

_____

7. While hiking through the state park, many animals can be seen.

_____

People—not animals—are the ones who are hiking through the state park.

8. Tossing trash out the window, the teenagers' car was stopped by the police.

_____

Name _____   Section _____   Date _____
Score: (Number right) _____ × 12.5 = _____ %

■ Misplaced and Dangling Modifiers: Test 2

In each sentence, underline the one misplaced or dangling modifier. (The first four sentences contain misplaced modifiers; the second four sentences contain dangling modifiers.) Then rewrite each sentence so that its intended meaning is clear.

1. I had a big lunch today, so I hardly ate anything for dinner.

   _____

2. The children placed their soup on the windowsill, which was too hot to eat.

   _____

   _____

3. The instructor told the students to sit down in a loud voice.

   _____

   _____

4. Residents of the burning house were carried out by firemen wearing only pajamas.

   _____

   _____

5. Involved in a noisy game of Monopoly, the summer evening together was enjoyable for us.

   _____

   _____

6. Growing thinner every day, Albert's diet is really working.

   _____

   _____

7. Whining and twitching, the dog's dream must have been about chasing rabbits.

   _____

   _____

8. Unable to read yet, my mother explained that the sign said, "No children allowed."

   _____

   _____

Name _____   Section _____ Date _____

■ Misplaced and Dangling Modifiers: Test 3

Each group of sentences contains one misplaced and one dangling modifier. Underline these errors. Then, on the lines provided, rewrite the parts of the sentences that contain the errors so that the intended meanings are clear.

Note   To help you correct misplaced and dangling modifiers, explanations are given for the first error in each group.

1. Will was disappointed when he looked in the refrigerator. There had been lots of spaghetti last night. His roommates, however, almost had eaten all of it. Frowning angrily, nothing but a few strands of spaghetti were left.

    a. _____
    The sentence suggests that the roommates *didn't* eat the spaghetti. Actually, they did eat most of it.

    b. _____

2. Lani stopped to watch the sidewalk artist with amazement. He was drawing a pencil portrait of a little girl. Sketching quickly, the portrait took shape under the artist's careful hand. "What remarkable talent," Lani commented.

    a. _____
    Lani, not the artist, is the one who is amazed.

    b. _____

3. I lost my raincoat last fall. I thought I'd looked everywhere for it. Then, yesterday, stuffed under the bed, I spotted it. Wrinkled and dusty, I was still delighted.

    a. _____
    The intended meaning is that the *raincoat*—not the speaker—was under the bed.

    b. _____

4. The sky was blue and clear when we arrived home. Only minutes later, though, there was a sudden crash of thunder. Rushing like mad, the windows in the bedrooms were closed. Staring out at the downpour, we were glad to be safe inside. Then we remembered our open car windows, groaning with dismay.

    a. _____
    Rushing like mad seems to be describing the windows.

    b. _____

■ Misplaced and Dangling Modifiers: Test 4

Each group of sentences contains one misplaced and one dangling modifier. Under-line these errors. Then, on the lines provided, rewrite the parts of the sentences that contain the errors so that the intended meanings are clear.

1. Going to camp was a nightmare for me. Being afraid of water, swimming was a frightening experience. I got a terrible case of poison ivy all over my legs, which seemed to be everywhere at the camp. I always remembered my time at camp as the longest week of my life.

   a. _____

   b. _____

2. Lana watched her twin sons toss a baseball back and forth through her living-room picture window. It was almost dinnertime. Shouting happily to each other, she knew their game of catch would soon have to end.

   a. _____

   b. _____

3. "I'd like to meet the girl who works in the snack shop with the red hair," said Vince. "Do you mean my cousin Helen? I can introduce you," his friend Tony replied. Pleased and excited, the meeting was soon arranged.

   a. _____

   b. _____

4. Cold and hungry, the street seemed a cruel place. People passing by ignored the homeless man completely. He watched them talking and laughing, sitting on the sidewalk in his thin sweater. "When I get out of this mess, I'm never going to ignore another street person again," he promised himself.

   a. _____

   b. _____

Name _____   Section _____   Date _____

Score: (Number right) _____ × 12.5 = _____ %

■ Misplaced and Dangling Modifiers: Test 5

Eight of the sentences in the following passage contain a misplaced or dangling modifier. Underline each modifier you believe to be misplaced or dangling, and then rewrite the parts of the sentences that contain the errors so that the intended meanings are clear.

Note   To help you correct misplaced and dangling modifiers, explanations are given for four of the sentences.

Ted and Linda decided to give their friend Garry a surprise birthday party that he would never forget. Working hard to make everything perfect, their menu was planned weeks in advance. They ordered a beautiful cake from a bakery with thirty-five candles. They bought five flavors of ice cream for the party, which they hid in the freezer. They scattered dozens of colorful balloons around the house, which they filled with helium. Finally, excited and pleased with all they had done, the guests were eagerly awaited. Linda saw people starting to arrive through the window. However, Garry was nowhere in sight. Suddenly, with a gasp, Ted realized that he had forgotten to bring the guest of honor. Rushing off in search of Garry, the party finally started—an hour late. "This party was supposed to only be a surprise for Garry," Ted said to the crowd, "but it turned out to be surprising for us as well."

1. _____

   The words *working hard to make everything perfect* apply to Ted and Linda, not to their menu.

2. _____

3. _____

   The writer means that the ice cream—not the party—was hidden in the freezer.

4. _____

5. _____

   Ted and Linda, not the guests, are the ones who were excited and pleased.

6. _____

7. _____

   The words *Rushing off in search of Garry* seem to be describing the party, but they really are about Ted.

8. _____

Name _____ Section _____ Date _____

Score: (Number right) _____ × 12.5 = _____%

■ Misplaced and Dangling Modifiers: Test 6

Eight of the sentences in the following passage contain a misplaced or dangling modifier. Underline each misplaced or dangling modifier. Then rewrite the parts of the sentences that contain the errors so that the intended meanings are clear.

    The Simpsons is the longest-running prime-time animated show in American television history. Presented for the first time on the Fox Network in 1989, millions of American homes have tuned in faithfully every Sunday evening for more than 20 years. *The Simpsons* is a satiric comedy about a dysfunctional family living in a small town of five members. Naming the characters after his own parents and siblings, Matt Groening's fictional Simpson family was originally created for a skit on *The Tracey Ullman Show*. Later, Groening gave the Simpsons their own series, in which he makes fun of many aspects of American society. Homer, the dim-witted father, works as a safety inspector at the Springfield Nuclear Power Plant. Playing the role of a stereotypical housewife, Marge's trademark is her large blue beehive hairdo. Bart, the oldest child, is the mischievous member of the family. At the beginning of each episode, he can be seen writing about his latest prank at the classroom chalkboard. He loves to annoy his serious sister Lisa by reacting to her good causes with insults. Always seen with a pacifier in her mouth, viewers wonder when they'll hear baby Maggie's first words. The show's success led to a full-length *Simpsons Movie* in 2007, which almost earned $600 million. In 2000, the Simpson family was honored with its own star on the Hollywood Walk of Fame.

1. _____

2. _____

3. _____

_____

4. _____

5. _____

6. _____

7. _____

8. _____

16 Parallelism

Seeing What You Know

Underline the part of each sentence that is not balanced—because it does not match other parts of the sentence. Then read the explanations that follow.

1. The manager is competent, good-natured, and offers help.

2. To lick water off the shower curtain, climbing up the side of the house, and sleeping in the kitchen sink are some of my cat's strange habits.

3. The expensive restaurant served overcooked fish, clam chowder that was cold, and half-melted ice cream.

4. No matter what his doctor tells him, Grady still smokes cigars, drinks heavily, and is staying out late at night.

Understanding the Answers

1. *Offers help* is the unbalanced portion of the sentence.
   Change it to *helpful* to match *competent* and *good-natured*.

2. *To lick water off the shower curtain* is out of balance.
   Change it to *Licking water off the shower curtain* to match *climbing up the side of the house* and *sleeping in the kitchen sink*.

3. *Clam chowder that was cold* does not match the rest of the sentence.
   Change it to *cold clam chowder* to give it the same form as the other two dishes—*overcooked fish* and *half-melted ice cream*.

4. *Is staying out late at night* is the unbalanced portion of the sentence.
   Change it to *stays out late at night* so that it has the same form as the other two parts of the list: *smokes cigars* and *drinks heavily*.

Two or more equal ideas should be expressed in **parallel**, or matching, form. The ideas will then read smoothly and naturally.

CORRECTING FAULTY PARALLELISM

Faulty parallelism is jarring and awkward to read. Consider this example:

Not parallel: The bowl was filled with **crisp apples**, **juicy oranges**, and **bananas that were ripe**.

In *crisp apples* and *juicy oranges,* the descriptive word comes first and the word being described comes second. In *bananas that were ripe,* the order is reversed.
    To achieve parallelism, give the nonparallel item the same form as the others:

Parallel: The bowl was filled with crisp apples, juicy oranges, and **ripe bananas**.

Now, the listed items are expressed in parallel form: *crisp apples, juicy oranges,* and *ripe bananas.*
    Here are additional examples of problems with parallelism and explanations of how to correct them:

Not parallel: My neighbor likes **to plant a garden**, **watering it**, and even **to weed it**.

    To plant a garden and *to weed it* are similar in construction, but *watering it* is not. For parallel construction, another *to* is needed.

Parallel: My neighbor likes to plant a garden, **to water it**, and even to weed it.

Not parallel: Would you prefer to spend the morning **playing basketball**, **watching television**, or **at the mall**?

    The word groups *playing basketball* and *watching television* both are *-ing* constructions, so *at the mall* needs an *-ing* word.

Parallel: Would you prefer to spend the morning **playing basketball**, **watching television**, or **shopping at the mall**?

Not parallel: The moviegoers **talked** and **were rattling** popcorn boxes during the film.

    Talked, an *-ed* construction, is not parallel to *were rattling.* The problem could be corrected by changing either word group.

Parallel: The moviegoers **talked** and **rattled** popcorn boxes during the film.

Also parallel: The moviegoers *were talking* and *were rattling* popcorn boxes during the film.

Practice 1

Cross out the one item in each list below that is not parallel in form to the other two items. Then, in the space provided, write the parallel form for that item.

1. to gather information
   to write several drafts
   printing the final copy

   _____

2. couple argued
   neighbors listened
   crying baby

   _____

3. wide-brimmed hat
   sunglasses that are dark
   protective sunscreen

   _____

4. managing an office
   sales representative
   telephone operator

   _____

5. selfish
   impatient
   lacking kindness

   _____

6. teaches social studies
   is coach of the track team
   runs the teachers' union

   _____

Practice 2

The part of each sentence that is not parallel is italicized. On the line, rewrite this part to make it match the other items listed.

1. The young boy, who is very talented, can sing, dance, and *knows how to play the piano.* _____

2. The most popular items on the buffet table were *shrimp that were steamed,* barbecued wings, and marinated steak tips. _____

3. Fall styles include wide-legged pants, short-cropped jackets, and *boots with high heels.* _____

4. Their intelligence, playfulness, and *being friendly* make dolphins appeal to people of all ages. _____

5. The crane's claws cradled the telephone pole, lifted it high overhead, and *were depositing it in the deep hole.* _____

WHEN TO USE PARALLELISM

Parallelism always applies to two or more *equal* ideas. Here are some writing situations in which parallelism is appropriate:

1 Presenting a series of items.

Popular summer vacation activities include **visiting** relatives, **hiking** in state parks, and **spending** time at the beach.

2   Offering choices.

The instructor announced that each student in the class could either **write a ten-page report** or **take the final exam**.

3   Making a point effectively.

Many famous speeches and pieces of writing feature skillful parallelism. The balance of their words and phrases helps make them memorable. For example,

"**Ask not what** your country can do for you; **ask what** you can do for your country." —*President John F. Kennedy*

Would Kennedy's speech have had the same ring if he'd said, "Don't ask what your country can do for you. Instead, you should be asking what you can do for your country"?

In his famous "I Have a Dream" speech, Dr. Martin Luther King, Jr., said he hoped that someday America would judge his children not "**by the color of their skin** but **by the content of their character**."

Dr. King's words gain power because they balance "the color of their skin" with "the content of their character." They would have been much less forceful if he had said instead, "Not by the color of their skin but according to how good a person each one is."

Practice 3

In the space provided, complete each list by adding a parallel item.

1. Three things I could not live without are my cell phone, my morning coffee, and _____.

2. To get the best buy on an appliance, compare brands, visit several stores, and _____.

3. At the adult evening school, I could sign up for a course in ballroom dancing, aerobic exercising, or _____.

4. "I still need a number of volunteers," the park director said, "to rake leaves, pick up trash, and _____."

5. Members of the work crew spent their lunch break eating sandwiches, napping on the grass, and _____.

Name _____   Section _____   Date _____

■ Parallelism: Test 1

Underline the part of each sentence below that upsets the sentence's parallelism. Then, in the space provided, rewrite the nonparallel item so that it matches the other item or items listed.

Note   To help you master the technique of parallelism, directions are given for half of the sentences.

1. Hawaii is famous for its beaches that are beautiful, warm climate, and exotic atmosphere.

_____

Beaches that are beautiful is the unbalanced part of the sentence. It needs to be changed to the same form as *warm climate* and *exotic atmosphere.*

2. Before leaving for work, Teresa exercises, eats breakfast, and the dog is fed.

_____

3. A wrecked car and breaking a collarbone were the results of the accident.

_____

Breaking a collarbone should be made parallel to *A wrecked car.*

4. Their father's gentleness and the sense of humor of their mother were two things that the children missed after they left home.

_____

5. Although the boss is smart, has good looks, and wealthy, he is coldhearted.

_____

Has good looks upsets the sentence's parallelism. It needs to be changed to the same form as *smart* and *wealthy.*

6. Even though Laila and Omar both loved to dance, enjoyed similar movies, and they shared some of the same friends, their blind date was not a success.

_____

7. Three remedies for an upset stomach are antacid pills, a diet that is bland, and flat ginger ale.

_____

A diet that is bland is out of balance. It needs to match *antacid pills* and *flat ginger ale.*

8. With her long legs, movements that are graceful, and pulled-back hair, the young woman looks like a ballerina.

_____

Name _____   Section _____   Date _____

                                              Score: (Number right) _____ × 10 = _____%

■ Parallelism: Test 2

Underline the part of each sentence below that upsets the sentence's parallelism. Then, in the space provided, rewrite the nonparallel item so that it matches the other item or items listed.

1. At the International Food Festival, visitors tasted tortillas, snacked on suki- yaki, and were munching on manicotti.

   _____

2. As the students waited for their instructor to arrive for class, they rummaged through their backpacks, were silencing their cell phones, and talked quietly to each other.

   _____

3. The ragged woman said she needed a meal, to have warm clothes, and a job.

   _____

4. You'll always be happy if you have your health, a loving family, and your work is satisfying.

   _____

5. The Harborside Restaurant offers delicious food, good service, and prices that are reasonable.

   _____

6. Making promises is easy; to keep them is hard.

   _____

7. The public relations position includes handling customers' complaints, keeping in touch with clients, and to write marketing material.

   _____

8. Because she missed her friend and wanting her to visit, Juanita telephoned her with an invitation.

   _____

9. Every year at the family barbecue, we choose teams and are playing touch football.

   _____

10. The professor suggested dropping the course or to get extra tutoring.

    _____

■ Parallelism: Test 3

Each group of sentences contains **two** errors in parallelism. Underline these errors. Then, on the lines below, rewrite the unbalanced portion to make it parallel with the other listed items in the sentence.

Note   To help you master the technique of parallelism, directions are given for half of the sentences.

1. Online dating is popular, unpredictable, and it can be risky. You never know if the person you've met online is telling the truth or used someone else's photo.

   a. _____   *It can be risky* must parallel
   b. _____   *popular* and *unpredictable.*

2. Good teachers, a modern facility, and students who are hardworking have all given the high school an excellent reputation. The school replaced two smaller schools that were known as places where teachers were third-rate, shabby described the buildings, and students were frustrated.

   a. _____   (*Students who are hardworking* must parallel
   b. _____   *good teachers* and *a modern facility.*)

3. My sister is a terrific athlete. She enjoys tennis, plays volleyball, and even rock climbing. I, on the other hand, find it challenging enough to climb stairs, walk around the block, or running for a bus.

   a. _____   (*Plays volleyball* must parallel *tennis* and
   b. _____   *rock climbing.*)

4. With her long black hair, eyes that are sparkling and dark, and tall, slim body, Regina looks like a fashion model. But she worries that no one notices her intelligence and hard work. Regina wants people to know that a woman can have beauty, ambition, and be intelligent, too.

   a. _____   (*Eyes that are sparkling and dark* needs to
   b. _____   parallel *long black hair* and *tall, slim body.*)

5. Working conditions at the factory were poor: loud machinery, conversations that were shouted, and blaring radios. Workers also complained about the low pay and the hours were long.

   a. _____   (*Conversations that were shouted* must
   b. _____   parallel *loud machinery* and *blaring radios.*)

Name _____ Section _____ Date _____

Score: (Number right) _____ × 10 = _____ %

■ Parallelism: Test 4

Each group of sentences contains **two** errors in parallelism. Underline these errors. Then, on the lines below, rewrite the unbalanced portion to make it parallel with the other listed items in the sentence.

1. Everything seemed to go wrong on Tuesday. My car broke down, my girlfriend not calling, and I locked myself out of my apartment. Besides, I had a sore throat, a headache, and my stomach ached.

   a. _____

   b. _____

2. I never spend money on fancy wrapping paper. When people get a present, they generally want to rip off the paper and be looking at what's inside. So I wrap my gifts in either plain brown grocery bags or Sunday comics that are colorful.

   a. _____

   b. _____

3. The symptoms of diabetes often include extreme thirst, hunger, and losing weight. The need to urinate frequently can also be a sign of the disease. If untreated, diabetes can lead to kidney and heart failure, the person going into a coma, and death.

   a. _____

   b. _____

4. My New Year's resolutions are to stop smoking, to study harder, and getting more involved in campus activities. On the other hand, my wife has resolved to eat more chocolate, exercising less, and to spend more time buying things on eBay.

   a. _____

   b. _____

5. The woman had ordered a large head of lettuce, green beans that were fresh, and ripe strawberries. The delivery man arrived with a head of cabbage that was tiny, frozen yellow beans, and sour red cherries.

   a. _____

   b. _____

Name _____   Section _____   Date _____

Score: (Number right) _____ × 10 = _____ %

■ Parallelism: Test 5

Ten of the sentences in the passage below contain errors in parallelism. Underline the errors and write in the numbers of the sentences that contain the errors. Then rewrite the nonparallel portion of each sentence in the space provided.

Note . To help you master the technique of parallelism, directions are given for half of the sentences.

[1]One summer Lynn worked as a student intern at her city's newspaper. [2]Although she was young, didn't have much experience, and nervous, she did well at her job. [3]Her cheerful attitude, willingness to work hard, and having the ability to get along with her coworkers impressed her editor. [4]Lynn did some of everything: she wrote up traffic accidents and weddings, was covering a few meetings, and even helped the photographer in the darkroom.

[5]One day her editor said, "Lynn, our police reporter needs an assistant. [6]Why don't you spend a few days following him around and see how you like it?" [7]Ozzie, the police reporter, explained to Lynn that he spent much of his time talking with police officers, visited crime scenes, and interviewing victims and witnesses. [8]Since she had always been interested in police work and liking Ozzie, Lynn was pleased with her new assignment. [9]At first she just trailed Ozzie around, took notes, and was asking a lot of questions. [10]One evening at home, however, as Lynn was straightening up her apartment and her plants were watered, Ozzie appeared at her door. [11]"Grab your notebook and camera—we're going on a raid," he yelled.

[12]Lynn dropped everything and was racing for Ozzie's car. [13]Soon they were speeding toward the address Ozzie had: a campground that had been closed for years. [14]Expecting a drug raid, the reporters were surprised to find dozens of police officers there breaking up an illegal cockfight operation. [15]Lynn and Ozzie began photographing the dead and wounded roosters and to question the gamblers. [16]As they drove back to the newspaper office late that night, Lynn said to Ozzie, "My college courses can teach me how to write, how to take pictures, and interviewing people. [17]But they could never prepare me for a crazy night like this."

1. *Sentence* ____: _____   (Parallel *young* and *nervous*)

2. *Sentence* ____: _____

3. *Sentence* ____: _____   (Parallel *wrote up* and *helped*)

4. *Sentence* ____: _____

5. *Sentence* ____: _____   (Parallel *she had always been interested*)

6. *Sentence* ____: _____

7. *Sentence* ____: _____   (Parallel *straightening up her apartment*)

8. *Sentence* ____: _____

9. *Sentence* ____: _____   (Parallel *photographing the dead and wounded roosters*)

10. *Sentence* ____: _____

Name _____   Section _____   Date _____

Score: (Number right) _____ × 10 = _____ %

■ Parallelism: Test 6

Ten of the sentences in the passage below contain errors in parallelism. Underline the errors, and write in the numbers of the sentences that contain the errors. Then rewrite the nonparallel portion of each sentence in the space provided.

¹"Reduce, Reuse, Recycle" is a slogan that can help you conserve energy. ²The slogan means that you should use as little as possible, use a product again if you can, and then recycling it. ³You can apply the "Reduce, Reuse, Recycle" principle at home, in your community, and where you work.

⁴"Reuse" and "Recycle" should be self-explanatory, but "Reduce" needs explaining. ⁵If you live where the weather is very hot or in a cold climate, good insulation can reduce the energy needed to maintain a comfortable temperature in your home. ⁶You can also adjust your thermostat, especially for times when you are sleeping or on a trip. ⁷You can further reduce energy usage if you unplug appliances, turn off lights, and by setting computers to go into sleep mode. ⁸You can reduce the amount of water you use—and the energy to heat it—by taking short showers and wash your dishes or clothes only when you have a full load. ⁹Better yet, you can wash dishes or clothes by hand. ¹⁰You can use less gasoline if you walk, bike, carpool, or public transportation. ¹¹All these measures are likely to save you money as well as saving energy.

¹²Shopping provides added opportunities for conserving energy. ¹³First, you will use less energy if you shop efficiently and making fewer trips to the store. ¹⁴You can also support energy conservation by purchasing products that are grown or manufactured close to your home and from stores that follow sound energy conservation policies themselves.

1. *Sentence* ____: _____

2. *Sentence* ____: _____

3. *Sentence* ____: _____

4. *Sentence* ____: _____

5. *Sentence* ____: _____

6. *Sentence* ____: _____

7. *Sentence* ____: _____

8. *Sentence* ____: _____

9. *Sentence* ____: _____

10. *Sentence* ____: _____

Part Two

Extending the Skills

Preview

Part Two presents some topics not included in Part One:

It also includes additional information about many of the topics presented in Part One:

17 Paper Form

Your instructor will probably give you specific directions for how your paper should look. However, the following guidelines normally apply:

1 Use 8.5- by 11-inch white paper.

2 Write or type on only one side of the paper.

3 Leave margins on all four sides of each page (1 to 1.5 inches is standard).

4 Put your name, the date, the course number, and, if required, your instructor's name where you have been told to put them—either at the top of page 1 or on a separate title page.

5 Put your title on the top line of the first page. Center it. Do not use quotation marks or underline your title. Capitalize the first word of the title as well as its other important words. (In the middle of a title, do not capitalize *a, an, the,* or prepositions such as *of, in, on, for, from, about, between*, and so on.) Skip a line between the title and the first sentence of your paper.

6 Ideally, prepare your paper on a computer. But if you are writing by hand,

   a Use blue or black ink—never pencil.

   b Use wide-lined paper, or write on every other line of narrow-lined paper.

   c Leave spaces between words. Also, leave a bit more space between sentences.

   d Make punctuation marks and capital letters clear and easy to read.

   e Write as neatly and legibly as you can.

7 Indent the first line of each paragraph one-half inch from the left-hand margin. Do not indent when starting a new page—unless you are also starting a new paragraph.

8 If a word will not fit at the end of a line, hyphenate it (divide it with a hyphen) only between syllables. Do not divide a one-syllable word.

9 Make sure your pages are in the correct order, numbered (except for page 1), and fastened.

10 Proofread your paper carefully before handing it in. Neatly correct any errors you find. Recopy or print a new copy of the paper if you discover a great many errors.

Practice

Following are the title and the first paragraph of a paper. Copy the title (adding capital letters where needed) and as much of the paragraph as will fit into the model of lined paper below. Use the guidelines above.

Information for the paper:

Title: community service in the 21st century

Soon after becoming president, Barack Obama urged Americans to follow his example and look for ways to serve their communities. Many people, inspired by his words, have volunteered in local and national programs. The idea is a good one for several reasons. Service programs create job opportunities for people of all ages. Such programs help America solve problems in all types of neighborhoods. Finally, community service brings us together as a people.

18 Spelling

The following hints will help even a poor speller become a better one.

1   **Use spelling aids.** These include a dictionary, a spelling-checker on a computer or electronic typewriter, and pocket-size electronic spell-checkers.

2   **Keep a personal spelling list.** Write down every word you misspell. Include its correct spelling, underline the difficult part of the word, and add any hints you can use to remember how to spell it. You might even want to start a spelling notebook that has a separate page for each letter of the alphabet. Here's one format you might use (another is on the inside back cover of this book):

How I spelled it	Correct spelling	Hints
recieve	rec*e*ive	I before E except after C.
seperate	sep*a*rate	There's A RAT in sepARATe.

Study your list regularly, and refer to it whenever you write or proofread a paper.

3   **Learn commonly confused words.** Many spelling errors result from confusing words like *to* and *too, its* and *it's, where* and *were.* Study carefully the pairs of words on pages 144–146 and 223–225.

4   **Apply basic spelling rules.** Here are four rules that usually work. The first rule will help you spell *ie* and *ei* words. The last three rules refer to adding endings.

I before E rule: I before E except after C
    Or when sounded like A, as in *neighbor* and *weigh.*

Examples: bel**ie**ve, ch**ie**f, rec**ei**ve, c**ei**ling, th**ei**r
Exceptions: **ei**ther, l**ei**sure, s**ei**ze, sc**ie**nce, soc**ie**ty, for**ei**gn

Silent E rule: If a word ends in a silent (unpronounced) *e,* drop the *e* before an ending that starts with a vowel. Keep the *e* before an ending that begins with a consonant.

Examples: hope + ed = ho**p**ed   guide + ance = gui**d**ance
    confuse + ing = confu**s**ing   love + ly = lov**e**ly
    fame + ous = fa**m**ous   care + ful = car**e**ful

Exceptions: peac**e**able, tr**u**ly, arg**u**ment, jud**gm**ent

Y rule: Change the final *y* of a word to *i* when

    a The last two letters of the word are a consonant plus *y.*
    b The ending being added begins with a vowel or is *-ful,
    -ly,* or *-ness.*

> ***But:*** Keep a *y* that follows a vowel. Also, keep the *y* if the ending being added is *-ing*.

Examples:
fly+ es = fli**es**	happy + ness = happ**i**ness
try + ed = tr**ie**d	destroy + s = destro**y**s
beauty + ful = beaut**i**ful	display + ed = displa**y**ed
lucky + ly = luck**i**ly	carry + ing = carr**y**ing

Exceptions: paid, said, laid, daily

Doubling rule: Double the final consonant of a word when

a The last three letters of the word are a consonant, a vowel, and a consonant (CVC).

b The word is only one syllable (for example, *stop*) or is accented on the last syllable (for example, *begin*).

c The ending being added begins with a vowel.

Examples:
stop + ed = sto**pp**ed	hot + er = ho**tt**er
begin + ing = begi**nn**ing	red + est = re**dd**est
control + er = contro**ll**er	occur + ence = occu**rr**ence

Note   With amazing frequency, students misspell the words *a lot* and *all right*. In each case they incorrectly combine the words to form one word: *alot* and *alright*. Remember that both *a lot* and *all right* are two words!

Practice

Use the preceding rules to spell the ten words that follow.

 1. (Add the ending)   party + s =   _____

 2. (Add the ending)   refer + ed =   _____

 3. (Add the ending)   write + ing =   _____

 4. (Add the ending)   definite + ly =   _____

 5. (Write *ie* or *ei*)   dec_____ve

 6. (Add the ending)   employ + er =   _____

 7. (Add the ending)   admit + ance =   _____

 8. (Add the ending)   marry + ing =   _____

 9. (Write *ie* or *ei*)   fr_____ndly

10. (Add the ending)   pity + ful =   _____

19 Pronoun Types

Personal Pronouns

Subject Pronouns

Subject pronouns function as subjects of verbs. These are the subject pronouns:

| I | you | he | she | it | we | they |

Here are some examples of subject pronouns in sentences:

He can resolve the problem. (*He* is the subject of the verb *can resolve*.)

You and **she** had a fight. (*You* and *she* are the ones who had a fight.)

It was **I** who called you.
(Use a subject pronoun after a form of the verb *be—am, are, is, was, were, has been,* etc.)

I'm as hungry as **they**.
(This means, "I'm as hungry as they *are*." *They* is the subject of the suggested verb *are*.)

Object Pronouns

Object pronouns serve as the objects of verbs (receivers of the verbs' action) or of prepositions (the last words in prepositional phrases). Here are the object pronouns:

| me | you | him | her | it | us | them |

Here are examples of object pronouns in sentences:

The children had wandered away, but their father finally found **them**. (*Them* receives the action of the verb *found*.)

The teacher gave a retest to José and **me**. (*Me* is the object of the preposition *to*.)

Hint   If a sentence is about two people and you aren't sure which pronoun to use, try using each pronoun by itself. Then choose the pronoun that sounds correct. For example, you would say, "The teacher gave a retest to me," not "to I."

Possessive Pronouns

Possessive pronouns show ownership or possession. Here are the possessive pronouns:

| *Singular:* | my, mine | your, yours | his | her, hers | its |
| *Plural:* | our, ours | your, yours | | their, theirs | |

Here are examples of possessive pronouns in sentences:

José got an A on **his** retest, but I got only a B on **mine**. (*His* refers to José's test; *mine* refers to my test.)

There are two points to remember about possessive pronouns:

1   Possessive pronouns never contain an apostrophe.

The book Alice lent me is missing **its** cover (not *it's cover*).

2   Do not use a subject or object pronoun where a possessive is needed.

Could I borrow **your** notes (not *you notes*) before the exam?
My refrigerator (not *me refrigerator*) is out of order.

Relative Pronouns

Relative pronouns refer to someone or something already mentioned in the sentence. Relative pronouns include the following:

who   **whose**   **whom**   **which**   **that**

Here are some examples of relative pronouns in sentences:

A cousin **whom** I've never met is coming to visit me. (*Whom* refers to *cousin.*)

The drill **that** you want is in the basement. (*That* refers to *drill.*)

Dick saw an old classmate **whose** name he had forgotten. (*Whose* refers to *classmate.*)

Here are some rules to remember about relative pronouns:

1   *Whose* means *belonging to whom.* Don't confuse it with *who's,* which means *who is.* (See page 146.)

2   The pronouns *who* and *whom* refer to people. *Whose* usually refers to people but often refers to things ("The tree **whose** branches damaged our roof belongs to our neighbor"). *Which* refers to things. *That* can refer to either people or things.

3   *Who* is a subject pronoun; *whom* is an object pronoun.

I wonder **who** is at the door. (*Who* is the subject of the verb *is.*)

The clerk **whom** I asked couldn't help me. (*Whom* is the object of *asked.*)

Note   To determine whether to use *who* or *whom,* find the first verb after the place where the *who* or *whom* will go. Decide whether that verb already has a subject. If it lacks a subject, use the subject pronoun *who.* If it does have a subject, use the object pronoun *whom.*

My parents will accept any person (who, whom) I choose to marry.

Look at the verb *choose.* Does it have a subject? Yes, the subject is *I.* Therefore, the object pronoun *whom* is the correct choice: My parents will accept any person *whom* I choose to marry.

Demonstrative Pronouns

Demonstrative pronouns are used to point out one or more particular persons or things. These are the demonstrative pronouns:

Singular: **this**   **that**   *Plural:* **these**   **those**

This and *these* generally refer to things that are near the speaker; *that* and *those* refer to things farther away.

I like **this** better than **those**.

Don't ever say **that** to me again.

Note 1   Demonstrative pronouns can also be used as adjectives: **this** cake, **those** cookies, **that** word.

Note 2   Do not use *them, this here, that there, these here,* or *those there* to point out.

Reflexive and Intensive Pronouns

Singular: **myself**   **yourself**   **himself, herself, itself**
Plural: **ourselves**   **yourselves**   **themselves**

(Remember that the plural of *-self* is *-selves.* There is no such word as *ourself* or *themself.*)

A **reflexive pronoun** is the object of a verb or preposition in sentences in which that object is the same as the subject.

I gave **myself** a birthday present.
(The subject of the verb, *I,* is the same as the object of the verb, *myself.*)

In the shower, Dad talks out loud to **himself**.
(The subject of the sentence, *Dad,* is the same as the object of the preposition *to, himself.*)

An **intensive pronoun** emphasizes a noun or another pronoun.

I **myself** will tell the police what happened.

She has to do her schoolwork **herself**.

Interrogative Pronouns

Interrogative pronouns are used to ask questions. Here are common interrogative pronouns:

who   **whose**   **whom**   **which**   **what**

Here are examples of interrogative pronouns in sentences:

Who is downstairs?   **Which** road should we take?   **What** is the matter?

There are two points to remember about interrogative pronouns:

1   Choose *who* or *whom* in the same manner as you would for relative pronouns.

Whom should I pick for the team?
(*I* is the subject of *should pick,* so use *whom.*)

Who tries hardest?
(The verb after *who* is *tries,* which does not have a subject. Therefore, use the subject form of the word, *who.*)

2   *Whose* is the possessive form of *who. Who's* means *who is.*

Whose turn is it?   **Who's** bringing the sodas?

Indefinite Pronouns

Indefinite pronouns do not refer to specific persons or things. Most of them are singular:

one	**none**	**each**	**either**
anyone	**someone**	**everyone**	**no one**
anybody	**somebody**	**everybody**	**nobody**
anything	**something**	**everything**	**nothing**

Some are plural:

both	**several**	**few**	**many**

Some can be either singular or plural:

all	**any**	**more**	**most**	**some**	**none**

Here are examples of indefinite pronouns in sentences. (See also pages 41–42.)

Somebody ate the last piece of chocolate cake. **None** of the cake is left.
Both of my sisters want to become police officers.
Most of the house has been painted. *(Singular; refers to one thing—the house)*
Most of the rooms need painting, too. *(Plural; refers to several things—the rooms)*

Practice

Underline the correct pronoun in each pair in parentheses.

1.   Are those (you, your) car keys on the kitchen table?

2.   All those dirty clothes on the closet floor are (hers, her's).

3.   Today the manager warned two coworkers and (I, me) about personal use of the copy machine.

4.   (He, Him) and (I, me) haven't seen each other in months.

5. Everyone else in my family is taller than (I, me).

6. (Them, Those) eggs are rotten.

7. (Who, whom) is going to get a bonus this year?

8. Are you going to eat (these, these here) corn chips?

9. It is (they, them) who will be sorry for what they (themself, themselves) have done.

10. All the people (who, whom) we asked for directions turned out to be just as lost as we were.

20 Adjectives and Adverbs

Identifying Adjectives

Adjectives are words that describe nouns (names of people, places, or things). An adjective can be found in two places in a sentence:

1 An adjective comes before the word it describes (a **loud** noise, a **wet** dog, the **oldest** child).

2 An adjective that describes the subject of a sentence may also come after a linking verb (see pages 6 and 19). The linking verb may be a form of the verb *be* (they are **delicious**, she is **pleased**, I am **sure**). Other linking verbs include *feel, look, sound, smell, taste, appear, seem, grow, remain,* and *become* (it seems **strange**, I feel **sick**, you look **happy**, it tastes **awful**).

Adjectives in Comparisons

Adjectives change form when they are used to make a comparison. Add *-er* to a short (usually one-syllable) adjective when you are comparing two things. Add *-est* when you are comparing three or more things.

> This green chili pepper is **hot**, but that red one is **hotter**.
>
> Of all the chili peppers I've ever tasted, that red one is the **hottest**.

With most adjectives that have two or more syllables, however, do not change the form of the adjective at all. Instead, use the word *more* when comparing two things and *most* when comparing three or more things.

> To me, David Letterman is **more entertaining** than Jay Leno, but Johnny Carson was the **most entertaining** of all.

Note 1 Do not use both an *-er* ending and *more,* or both an *-est* ending and *most.*

Incorrect: "This is the most happiest day of my life," Denise said.

Correct: "This is the **happiest** day of my life," Denise said.

Note 2 Certain short adjectives have irregular forms:

	Comparing two	*Comparing three or more*
bad	worse	worst
good, well	better	best
little	less	least
much, many	more	most

In my opinion, David Letterman's show is **better** than Jay Leno's, but Johnny Carson's was the **best**.

Identifying Adverbs

Adverbs are words that describe verbs, adjectives, and other adverbs. Most adverbs end in the letters *ly*. The following examples show how adverbs are used:

The clerk spoke to me **rudely**. (The adverb *rudely* tells how the clerk spoke.)

Colleen is **truly** sorry for her angry remark. (The adverb *truly* describes the adjective *sorry*; it tells how sorry Colleen is.)

The canary sings **very** sweetly. (The adverb *very* describes the adverb *sweetly*; it tells how sweetly the canary sings.)

Using Adverbs

Be careful to use an adverb—not an adjective—after an action verb. Compare the following:

Incorrect	*Correct*
The car runs good. (*Good* is an adjective, not an adverb)	The car runs **well**.
Listen careful to the directions. (*Careful* is an adjective)	Listen **carefully** to the directions.
She went to sleep quick. (*Quick* is an adjective.)	She went to sleep **quickly**.

Pay particular attention to the difference between the words *good* and *well*. *Good* is an adjective that often means "talented" or "positive":

Zoe is a **good** guitarist.
We had a **good** time.
Do you feel **good** about yourself?

As an adverb, *well* often means "skillfully" or "successfully":

She plays the guitar **well**.
He does his job **well**.
I did **well** on that project.

As an adjective, *well* means "healthy," as in the question "Are you feeling **well**?"

Practice

Cross out the incorrect adjective or adverb in each of the following sentences. Then write the correction on the line provided.

1. _____ Is psychology a more harder subject than sociology?

2. _____ To stay in good shape, exercise regular.

3. _____ Those three students did real well on the last exam.

4. _____ The most greatest challenge in my life is working and going to school at the same time.

5. _____ Of the two computers I tried last week, the Macintosh was easiest for me to use.

6. _____ Brenda spoke soft to the frightened puppy.

7. _____ I use lesser butter and sugar in my cooking than I used to.

8. _____ Always proofread the last version of your paper careful before handing it in.

9. _____ Cara didn't go to class today because she didn't feel good.

10. _____ After she took aspirin and cold medicine, Cara felt more better than she had before.

21 Numbers and Abbreviations

Numbers

Here are some guidelines to follow when writing numbers:

1   Spell out a number if it can be written in one or two words. Otherwise, write it in numerals.

The new high school has **three** vice principals, **ninety-five** teachers, and **two thousand** students.

There are **15,283** books in its library.

2   Spell out any number that begins a sentence.

Four hundred ninety-three people were in the first graduating class.

3   Be consistent when you write a series of numbers. If one or more numbers in the series need to be written as numerals, write *all* the numbers as numerals.

The carpenter bought **150** nails, **12** bolts, and **2** drill bits.

4   Use numerals to write dates, times, addresses, percentages, portions of a book, and exact amounts of money that include change.

The attorney asked the witness where she was on September **12, 2009**.

Set the alarm for **5:45** A.M. (When the word *o'clock* is used, however, the time is spelled out, as in *I get up at five o'clock.*)

The cabdriver took me to **418** East **78th** Street.

Only **30** percent of the students voted in the mock presidential election.

The test will cover Chapters **1**, **2**, and **3** in your textbook, pages **5–74**.

My monthly car payment is **$348.37**.

Abbreviations

In general, avoid using abbreviations in papers you write for class. The following are among the few abbreviations that are acceptable in formal writing.

1   Titles that are used with proper names (for example, *Mr., Mrs., Dr., Jr., Sr.*):

Mrs. Richardson   **Dr.** Bell   Edwin Sacks, **Jr.**   **Prof.** George Smith

2   Initials in a person's name:

J. Edgar Hoover   Edgar **A.** Poe

3   Time references (A.M., P.M., B.C., A.D.):

After the party, we didn't get to bed until 4 A.M.

4   Organizations, technical words, and trade names referred to by their initials. These are usually written in all capital letters and without periods:

FBI   CIA   IRS   AIDS   NAACP   UNICEF   YMCA

Practice

Cross out the mistake in number or abbreviation in each of the following sentences. Then write the correction on the line provided.

1. _____ This semester, Amahl is taking 5 classes and two labs.

2. _____ If only twenty-five percent of every paycheck didn't get taken out for taxes!

3. _____ The co. is taking job applications from 8:00 to 11:00 A.M.

4. _____ 150 members of the marching band spelled out "Victory!" in front of fifty thousand cheering fans.

5. _____ To earn my degree, I went to coll. for 4 years, took 40 courses, and wrote a 125-page thesis.

6. _____ Why are you setting the alarm for six A.M. if your first class isn't until eight o'clock?

7. _____ My dr. just told me that I had to lose fifteen pounds.

8. _____ On June seventh, 2012, Rasheed will finally be discharged from military duty.

9. _____ That prof. doesn't give you an A unless you score 94 percent or above.

10. _____ When Rachel opened the used book she had purchased, she saw that Chapter Ten (pages 89 through 102) had been torn out.

22 Usage

Here are some common incorrect expressions, together with their correct forms:

Incorrect	Correct
anyways, anywheres	anyway, anywhere
being as, being that	because, since
can't help but, cannot hardly, cannot scarcely (*double negatives*)	can't help, can hardly, can scarcely
could of, may of, might of, must of, should of, would of	could have, may have, might have, must have, should have, would have
had ought	ought
irregardless	regardless
kind of a	kind of
nowheres	nowhere
off of	off
suppose to, use to	supposed to, used to
sure and, try and	sure to, try to
the reason is because	the reason is that (See page 201.)
ways (meaning "distance")	way

Practice

Cross out the incorrect expression in each sentence. Then, on the line provided, rewrite that part of the sentence to eliminate the error in usage.

1. Every time I see the movie *Titanic,* I can't hardly keep from crying.

   _____

2. The instructor asked the class to try and finish the assignment by the following Monday.

   _____

3. Verna used to live a long ways from here, but now she's renting an apartment a few blocks away.

   _____

4. Since no one in this course understands the textbook, the instructor had ought to assign a different one.

   _____

5. Nobody could of known ahead of time how different college is from high school.

   _____

6. "Regardless of what you think," the counselor said, "you should of gone to class more often."

   _____

7. I couldn't help but notice that you're wearing a different kind of cologne.

   _____

8. Being that he has spent at least ten winters in Indiana, Bob ought to be used to cold weather.

   _____

9. "Take your muddy feet off of my sofa this minute!" Juanita screamed at her son. "You certainly should have known better than to do that!"

   _____

10. The driver pulled over to the curb and asked, "Is there a convenience store anywheres nearby?"

    _____

23 Mixed Constructions

Sometimes, by the time they reach the end of a sentence, writers forget how they started it. In these cases, the sentence can end up in a very different—and confusing—grammatical form. Sentences whose parts do not logically fit together are called **mixed constructions**.

To correct a mixed construction, do one of the following:

1 Turn the first part of the sentence into something that can be the subject.
Mixed: By practicing six hours a day helped Sasha become a champion skater.
Corrected: **Practicing six hours a day** helped Sasha become a champion skater.

2 Turn the second part of the sentence into a complete statement.
Mixed: Just because you got your learner's permit does not automatically give you permission to drive the car.
Corrected: Just because you got your learner's permit, **you do not automatically get permission to drive the car**.

Three Word Groups That Lead to Mixed Constructions

is when	is where	reason is because

Is (along with other forms of *to be*) is a linking verb. It needs to be followed by a subject complement (a noun), not a dependent word like *where, when,* or *because*. In definitions, or when giving examples, avoid using *is when* or *is where*.

Mixed: An approach-avoidance conflict is when someone is both attracted to and repelled by the same goal.
Corrected: An approach-avoidance conflict is **a situation in which** someone is both attracted to and repelled by the same goal.
Corrected: An approach-avoidance conflict **occurs when** someone is both attracted to and repelled by the same goal.

Mixed: Hawaii is where I have always wanted to go for a vacation.
Corrected: **I have always wanted to go to Hawaii** for a vacation.
Corrected: Hawaii is **the place where** I have always wanted to go for a vacation.

To correct *reason is because,* eliminate either *reason* or *because:*

Mixed: The reason Tanya was promoted is because she is a hard worker.
Corrected: **Tanya was promoted because** she is a hard worker.
Corrected: The reason Tanya was promoted is **that** she is a hard worker.

Practice

Rewrite each of the following sentences to eliminate the mixed construction.

1. The reason I got an A on the exam is because I studied my class notes.

   _____

   _____

2. Although that dog is ten years old, but he still runs around like a puppy.

   _____

   _____

3. By healthy eating and reducing portion sizes helped me lose twenty pounds.

   _____

   _____

4. When a recent immigrant applies for citizenship can take a long time.

   _____

   _____

5. For people who live alone often become depressed during the holiday season.

   _____

   _____

6. Revision is where a writer improves a paper by finalizing details, organizing clearly, and correcting spelling and grammar.

   _____

   _____

7. Kaylin set a new track record at her high school is why she was offered a scholarship.

   _____

   _____

8. At the beginning of the year is when students register for classes.

   _____

   _____

24 More about Subjects and Verbs

Sentences with More Than One Subject

A sentence may have a compound subject—in other words, more than one subject.

Ellen and **Karla** have started their own part-time business.

Sentences with More Than One Verb

A sentence may have a compound verb—in other words, more than one verb.

They **plan** parties for other people and also **provide** all the refreshments.

Sentences with More Than One Subject and Verb

A sentence may have both a compound subject and a compound verb.

In the last two weeks, **Ellen** and **Karla arranged** a wedding reception, **catered** a retirement dinner, and **earned** more than five hundred dollars.

Practice

In the sentences below, cross out any prepositional phrases. Then underline each subject once and each verb twice.

1. The catcher's mitt, skateboard, and pile of dirty laundry in the closet belong to my teenage son.

2. The car's motor coughed once and refused to start.

3. Accounting and computer science are very practical majors but require a lot of work.

4. Lisa tore the wrapping off the present, lifted the lid of the box, and gasped in delight.

5. The author of the popular children's book and her husband attended the book signing, sipped coffee, and chatted with visitors.

25 Even More about Verbs

Tense

Tense refers to time. The tenses of a verb tell us when the action of the verb took place. The twelve major tenses in English for the regular verb *look* are shown in the box that follows.

Twelve Verb Tenses		
Tense	*Time Referred To*	*Example*
Present	Happens now *or* happens habitually	I **look** good today. Miguel **looks** like his father.
Past	Already happened	Students **looked** the word up in the dictionary.
Future	Is going to happen	Things **will look** better for you in a few days.
Present perfect	Began in past and now completed or continuing in present	Corinne **has looked** much more relaxed since she changed jobs. Corinne **has looked** for a new job before.
Past perfect	Happened before another past action	She **had looked** very tired before she quit her old job.
Future perfect	Is going to happen before some other future action	Her former boss **will have looked** at 350 job applications by the end of the month.
Present progressive	Is in progress	Eli **is looking** for a new apartment right now. His parents **are looking**, too.
Past progressive	Was in progress	He **was looking** in their old neighborhood, but they **were looking** downtown.
Future progressive	Will be in progress	With rents so high, they probably **will be looking** for quite a while.
Present perfect progressive	Was in progress and still is	Flora **has been looking** at soap operas for the last two hours.
Past perfect progressive	Was in progress until recently	She **had been looking** at her study notes.
Future perfect progressive	Will be in progress until a set time in the future	Unless she gets back to work, she **will have been looking** at television until dinnertime.

Voice

Voice refers to the active or passive form of a verb. In the **active voice**, the action of the verb is done *by* the subject:

> *Active:* A police officer **took** the lost child home. (The police officer performed the action.)

In the **passive voice**, the action is done *to* the subject:

Passive: The lost child **was taken** home by a police officer. (The police officer performed the action, which was done to the child.)

In your own writing, you should normally use active verbs, which are more powerful than passive verbs. Use the passive voice, however, in situations where the doer of the action is not known or not important:

Passive: On the morning of Chen's wedding day, his car **was stolen**.

Passive: I **was promoted** last week.

Verbals

Verbals, formed from verbs, are used to name or describe people, places, and things. The three kinds of verbals are shown below.

Verbal	How Formed	Example and Comment
Infinitive	*To* plus a verb	The lost child began **to cry**. (Infinitives are used as adjectives, adverbs, or nouns. In the sentence above, *to cry* functions as a noun—the direct object of the verb *began*.)
Participle	Present: verb plus *-ing* Past: verb + *-ed* or irregular form	The **crying, frightened** child could not be comforted. (Participles are used as adjectives to describe a noun; here the adjectives *crying* and *frightened* describe the child.)
Gerund	verb plus *-ing*	**Crying** is sometimes very healthy. (Gerunds are used as nouns; here the noun *crying* is the subject of the sentence.)

Practice 1

On the line, write the indicated form of each verb in parentheses.

1. (gerund)   *(See)* _____ is *(believe)* _____.
2. (infinitive)   Peter Pan was determined never *(grow)* _____ up.

3. (present
   perfect)

That cat *(give)* _____ birth to five litters of kittens.

4. (future
   progressive)

In early October, many tourists *(travel)* _____ through New England, just when the trees *(display)*

_____ their most magnificent fall colors.

5. (passive)

Since the couple wanted to keep wedding costs low, the bride's gown was homemade, and the groom's tuxedo *(borrow)*

_____ from his uncle.

Three Troublesome Pairs of Irregular Verbs

	Basic Form	*Past Tense*	*Past Participle*
lie / lay	*Lie* means *rest* or *recline.*	lay	lain
	Lay means *put* or *place* something down.	laid	laid

My father likes to **lie** down and take an afternoon nap. Yesterday he **lay** on the living-room couch for two hours. He has sometimes **lain** there all afternoon without getting up.

Rico **lays** his wet towel anywhere in the house. This morning he **laid** it on a hot radiator. After he **had laid** it there, the towel began to steam.

	Basic Form	*Past Tense*	*Past Participle*
sit / set	*Sit* means *rest* or *take a seat.*	sat	sat
	Set means *put* something down or *prepare* something for use.	set	set

LaToya never **sits** down at a table to eat. Monday she **sat** at her desk to eat lunch. She **has sat** in front of the television to eat dinner every night this week.

My sister is the one who **sets** the family dinner table every day. She **has set** it in various ways, depending on what's for dinner. For instance, when we had Chinese food last week, she **set** the table with just napkins and chopsticks.

	Basic Form	Past Tense	Past Participle
rise / raise	*Rise* means *go up.*	rose	risen
	Raise means *lift* something up or *increase* it.	raised	raised

The sun **rises** every morning. Today it **rose** at 6:12 A.M. As soon as it **had risen**, trash trucks began clattering down the street.

Justine **raises** her hand a lot in class. This week, she **raised** her hand every time the instructor asked a question. Maybe she **has raised** her grade this way.

Practice 2

Underline the correct form of each verb in parentheses.

1. You look tired. Why don't you (sit, set) down and rest for a while?

2. Those old magazines have (lain, laid) in piles in our garage for years.

3. The accident victim was in such pain that she couldn't (rise, raise) her head.

4. Everyone in the stadium (rose, raised) to sing the national anthem.

5. The restaurant customer (lay, laid) a five-dollar bill on the table and said to the waiter, "This is yours if you can bring me my food in five minutes."

26 More about Subject-Verb Agreement

When compound subjects are joined by *or, nor, either . . . or, neither . . . nor,* or *not only . . . but also,* the verb agrees with the closer subject.

> Either clams or lobster **is** the featured special every Friday at the restaurant. (*Lobster,* a singular subject, is closer to the verb, so the singular form *is* is required.)

> Either lobster or clams **are** the featured special every Friday at the restaurant. (*Clams,* a plural subject, is closer to the verb, so the plural verb *are* is used.)

While most indefinite pronouns are always singular (*each, everyone, one, somebody,* etc.—see page 41), a few are not. The pronouns *both, several, many,* and *a few* are always plural and require plural verbs:

> Both of my uncles **play** the piano and **sing** professionally. A few of my cousins **are** also performers.

The pronouns *all, any, some, more, most,* and *none* are either singular or plural, depending on the words that follow them. If the words after them are singular, they are singular. If the words after them are plural, however, they are plural. Notice the examples.

> Some of the birthday cake **is** still on the table. (Since *cake* is singular, *some* is singular in this sentence. A singular verb, *is,* is needed.)

> Some of the party guests **are** not having any dessert. (*Guests* is plural, making *some* plural in this sentence. The plural verb *are* is appropriate here.)

Practice

Underline the subject or subjects of each sentence. Then fill in the verb in parentheses that agrees with the subject or subjects.

1. *(tastes, taste)* A few of the chocolates in the box _____ funny.

2. *(stays, stay)* Either Thelma or her mother _____ at home to care for Thelma's grandmother.

3. *(is, are)* Not only Carl but also his friends _____ working at the neighborhood food bank this weekend.

4. *(was, were)*   All of the students in the course _____ glad when it was over.

5. *(has, have)*   Neither the head coach nor his assistant coaches _____ yet been fired for supplying bodybuilding drugs to players.

6. *(needs, need)* Both of my good shirts _____ to be ironed.

7. *(has, have)*   Either the professor's lectures or the textbook _____ to be updated.

8. *(Is, Are)*   _____ any of the lemon chiffon pie still in the refrigerator?

9. *(Is, Are)*   _____ any of the other desserts still available?

10. *(seems, seem)* Since all of the desserts _____ to be gone, I'm going out for ice cream.

27 More about Run-Ons and Comma Splices

Other Methods of Correcting a Run-On or a Comma Splice

Run-ons and comma splices may be corrected by putting a **semicolon (;)** between the two complete thoughts. A semicolon is a stronger mark of punctuation than a comma; it can therefore be used to connect two complete thoughts.

Run-on:	Carmen has a broken foot she won't be doing any hiking this summer.
Corrected:	Carmen has a broken foot**;** she won't be doing any hiking this summer.
Comma splice:	Our history professor has the flu, half the class is sick as well.
Corrected:	Our history professor has the flu**;** half the class is sick as well.

Note   Use the semicolon only when the connection between the two complete thoughts is obvious.

Or you can use a **semicolon plus a transitional word** (also called an **adverbial connective** or a **conjunctive adverb**) **and a comma** to make the connection between the two complete thoughts even clearer:

Carmen has a broken foot**; therefore,** she won't be doing any hiking this summer.

Our history professor has the flu**; in fact,** half the class is sick as well.

Here are some other transitional words that may be used to correct a run-on or a comma splice:

Transitional Words		
afterward	however	nevertheless
also	in addition	now
as a result	indeed	on the other hand
besides	instead	otherwise
consequently	meanwhile	then
furthermore	moreover	thus

Words That May Lead to Run-Ons and Comma Splices

Pay special attention to your punctuation when you use the following two types of words. Since they often begin a new complete thought, they can be a signal to help you avoid writing a run-on or a comma splice.

1   Personal pronouns—*I, you, he, she, it, we, they.*

Run-on: We were tired of studying we took a break.
Corrected: We were tired of studying, **so** we took a break.

2   Transitional words such as *therefore, in fact,* and the words in the box above.

Comma splice: The air conditioning wasn't working, as a result, many
                          customers left the store.

Corrected: The air conditioning wasn't working**;** as a result, many
                          customers left the store.

Note   When the transitional word occurs in the middle of one complete thought, it is an interrupter and is set off by commas:

The air conditioning wasn't working; many customers**, as a result,** left the store.

Practice

Correct each of the following run-ons or comma splices by adding a semicolon. In some cases, the semicolon will take the place of a comma.

1. Traffic leaving the concert was horrible we finally squeezed out of the parking lot at midnight.

2. Working from home saves time and money however, it can be very lonely.

3. The family made sure all doors and windows were locked moreover, they turned the thermostat down before leaving the house.

4. Pedestrians are treated like royalty in London cars and buses stop to allow them to cross the street.

5. Many ads talk about new and improved products nevertheless, the label on the box is often all that is new.

6. Jenny couldn't afford to pay her rent consequently, she advertised in the paper for a roommate.

7. The waiters served soft drinks to the children, they offered wine to the adults.

8. Chipmunks have dug many holes in our yard now it looks like a miniature golf course.

9. We will have to leave for the game within ten minutes, otherwise, we will miss the kickoff.

10. Our dog barks too much, as a result, the landlord has refused to renew our lease.

28 More about the Comma

Short Introductory Material

Short introductory material need not be followed by a comma.

> On my return I found the children had cooked dinner.
>
> Next to the computer a pot of coffee was leaking.
>
> Afterward Martin was glad he had gotten the tattoo.

More about Interrupters

A word group that identifies another word in the sentence is actually not an interrupter. It is needed to make the sentence clear and should not be set off with commas.* For instance, look at the boldfaced words in the following sentences:

> The woman **who lives next door to me** just won a million dollars in the lottery.
>
> Alice Adams**, who lives next door to me,** just won a million dollars in the lottery.

In the first sentence, the boldfaced words are needed to identify the woman. Without them, we would not know who just won a million dollars. Since the words do not interrupt the sentence, we do not use commas. In the second sentence, however, we already know who won the million dollars. (It was Alice Adams.) In that case, the boldfaced words are not essential to the main message of the sentence. So, in the second sentence, *who lives next door to me* is an interrupter and should be set off by commas.

To find out whether a word group is an interrupter and should be set off by commas, try reading the sentence without it. The first sentence above would then read, "The woman just won a million dollars in the lottery." This version makes us ask, "Which woman?" The boldfaced words are needed to give us that information. If we read the second sentence without the boldfaced words, we would not be omitting essential information: "Alice Adams just won a million dollars in the lottery."

Other Joining Words

You already know that when two complete thoughts are combined into one sentence by a joining word like *and, but,* or *so,* a comma is used before the joining word. *Or, nor, for* (which means *because*), and *yet* (which means *however*) are also joining words. Put a comma before each of these words when it joins two complete thoughts.

---

*Grammar books sometimes refer to interrupters as "nonrestrictive elements" and essential descriptions as "restrictive elements."

Buyers may pay in advance, **or** they may choose the easy-payment plan.

Alonso did not want to read his paper aloud, **nor** did he want anyone else to read it for him.

All the houseplants died, **for** they hadn't been watered in weeks.

The home team was behind by seven runs, **yet** the fans remained in the stadium.

Other Uses of the Comma

1   Use a comma to set off short expressions (*yes, no, well,* and the like) at the beginnings or ends of sentences.

No, you may not borrow the car.

Would you step aside, please?

2   Use a comma to set off the name of a person spoken to.

Can't you sleep, Barry?

Mom, your skirt is too short.

Hey, mister, you forgot your change.

3   Use commas within a date or an address.

Friday, May 14, 2010, will be the last day of final exams. (Place commas after the day of the week, the date, and the year.)

Send your comments about *English Brushup* to McGraw-Hill, 2 Penn Plaza, New York, NY 10121.

Note   When you write an address in a sentence, place commas after the name (if included), the street address, and the city. Do not place a comma between the state and the ZIP code.

4   Place a comma after the opening and closing of an informal letter.

Dear Aunt Ruth,   Dear Mr. Ellis,   With love,   Sincerely,

Note   A colon is used after the opening of a business letter.

5   Place a comma between two descriptive words when they are interchangeable (in other words, when reversing their order would make sense).

Many people dream about taking a vacation from their stressful, demanding jobs. (We could just as easily say "demanding, stressful jobs," so a comma is needed.)

For some people, a fantasy vacation spot is a small tropical island. (We wouldn't say "a tropical small island," so the words are not reversible. No comma is used.)

Note   Another way to tell if two descriptive words need a comma is to see if the word *and* can be put between them. If so, a comma is used. "Stressful and demanding jobs" makes sense, so the comma is appropriate. "Small and tropical island" does not, so no comma is used.

Practice 1

Insert commas where needed in each of the following sentences.

1. Vanessa are you ready to give your report?
2. The letter was mailed on Monday morning yet it did not arrive until the following Saturday.
3. The official-looking form dated March 8 2010 said to report for jury duty to the Glendale Courthouse Front and Orange Streets Glendale CA 91208.
4. The confused angry man seemed to be yelling at nobody.
5. The man who came to the party with Joy says he was kidnapped by aliens.
6. Harvey who came to the party with Joy says he was kidnapped by aliens.
7. No you do not need an appointment to get a haircut.
8. Please wear your dark blue suit to the reception Sam.
9. I'm going to ask Alice for a loan for she has plenty of money to spare.
10. Dear Rhett

    I can't wait to see you! I'll be there to greet you when you step off the plane.

    With love
    Scarlett

When Not to Use a Comma

If no clear comma rule applies, it's better not to use a comma—"when in doubt, leave it out." Do not use a comma in the following situations:

Between a subject and verb:
A fast-moving storm, dumped a foot of snow onto our town last night.

Between a verb and its object:
The snow that fell completely covered, every road and bridge.

Before a prepositional phrase:
Salting crews and snowplow operators battled the storm, throughout the night.

Before *and* in a compound subject or compound verb:
Today workers, and shoppers reluctantly got up extra early, and tried to uncover their cars.

Before *that* (unless an interrupter follows):
The children happily slept late because they knew, that they had a day off from school.

Practice 2

In each sentence, cross out the **one** comma that does not belong there. Do not add any commas.

1. In the middle of the night, my cat jumped on the bed, and woke me up, but I went back to sleep again.

2. Yes, my friend, I can see, that you've lost a lot of weight.

3. Although taking the bus, which stops right at her corner, saves her money, Delia, prefers driving to work.

4. On Saturday, June 4, 2011, I will finally graduate, from community college.

5. Whenever I see, the commercial about the beautiful weather in Florida, I want to grab the TV, carry it to the window, and throw it onto my icy sidewalk.

29 More about the Apostrophe

Apostrophes in Special Plurals

Use an apostrophe and *s* to make each of the following plural:

Letters. Bert usually gets **C's** in math and science and **A's** in everything else. How many **e's** are there in *cemetery*?

Words used as words. The instructor told us not to use so many ***and's*** in our papers.

But To make a number plural, add only an *s*:

There are three **7s** in the store's telephone number.

Today's reality TV shows actually originated in the **1940s** and **1950s**.

When Not to Use an Apostrophe: Possessive Pronouns

Do not put an apostrophe in any of these possessive pronouns: *his, hers, its* (meaning *belonging to it*), *ours, yours, theirs.* Since they are already possessive, they do not need an apostrophe.

Incorrect	*Correct*
The baseball jackets are theirs'.	The baseball jackets are **theirs**.
One can sometimes tell a book by it's cover.	One can sometimes tell a book by **its** cover.
Are those car keys his' or your's?	Are those car keys **his** or **yours**?

Practice

Insert apostrophes where needed in each of the following sentences. (Not all of the sentences require the addition of apostrophes.)

1. When I write quickly, my 4s, 7s, and Ts look exactly alike.

2. Those packages are ours, but the shopping bags in the corner are hers.

3. Does a student need to have all As and Bs to graduate with honors?

4. Until the freshly varnished table has completely dried, its surface will be sticky.

5. What this world needs is more *pleases* and *thank-yous.*

30 More about Quotation Marks

Other Uses of Quotation Marks

1   Use single quotation marks to indicate a quotation within a quotation.

You've learned to use quotation marks to indicate someone's exact words or the title of a short work. When a second group of exact words or the title of a short work appears within a quoted passage, use single quotation marks to set it off.

Cal's boss told him, "If I hear you say 'That's not my job' one more time, you're not going to have any job at all."

"Let's join together and serenade our guest of honor with 'Happy Birthday,'" Enrique said.

2   Use quotation marks to set off words used in a special sense or words used as words.

The "major hurricane" we had all worried about turned out to be just a little rain and breeze.

Many people misspell the word "separate" as "seperate."

Note   In printed matter, *italics* are often used to indicate a word used as a word: The word *separate* contains the words *a rat*.

Quotation Marks and Other Punctuation

Periods and commas at the end of a quotation always go *inside* the quotation marks.

"Unless you're downstairs in three minutes," Lila said, "I'm leaving without you."

Semicolons and colons at the end of a quotation always go *outside* the quotation marks.

The speaker quoted the famous line from Langston Hughes's poem "Harlem": "What happens to a dream deferred?"

Question marks and exclamation points at the end of a quotation normally go *inside* the quotation marks. They go *outside* the quotation marks only if they apply to the entire sentence, not just the quoted part.

Lila asked, "How much longer are you going to take?" (The question mark applies only to what Lila said.)

Did Lila say, "I'm leaving without you"? (The question mark applies to the entire sentence.)

217

Practice

On the lines provided, rewrite each sentence, inserting quotation marks where needed.

1. For our next class, please read the short story The Yellow Wallpaper and write a journal entry about it, the instructor said.

   _____

   _____

2. I can't believe it—they just scored the winning basket with half a second remaining! the announcer gasped.

   _____

   _____

3. In which of Shakespeare's plays does a character say, To thine own self be true?

   _____

   _____

4. One of the longest words in the English language is antidisestablish-mentarianism.

   _____

   _____

5. Whenever I'm feeling depressed, my father always makes me smile by saying, Life is far too important to be taken seriously, Joanne said.

   _____

   _____

31 More about Punctuation Marks

Semicolon

Use a semicolon to set off items in a series when the items themselves contain commas.

At the family reunion I spent time talking with Uncle Ray, who is a retired train engineer; my cousin Cheryl, who works in publishing; and my nephew Walt, who plays violin in his high-school orchestra.

The radio station invited listeners to choose which of three songs should be named the greatest rock-and-roll classic of all time: "Hey, Jude," by the Beatles; "Satisfaction," by the Rolling Stones; or "Heartbreak Hotel," an Elvis Presley song.

Hyphen

1 Put a hyphen between the two parts of a fraction: one-half, two-thirds.

2 Hyphenate compound numbers from twenty-one to ninety-nine.

Hassan pays his parents eighty-seven dollars, one-fourth of his weekly salary, for room and board.

3 Use a hyphen after the prefixes *all-, ex-,* and *self-*.

Leaders should be self-confident, but they should never think they are all-powerful.

My ex-husband has started therapy to raise his self-esteem.

Dash

Use a dash to signal the end of a list of items.

A three-mile run, forty minutes of weight lifting, and seventy-five push-ups—that's how Grandfather starts his day.

Parentheses

Place parentheses around numbers that introduce items in a list within a sentence.

Grandfather's exercise program consists of (1) jogging, (2) weight lifting, and (3) push-ups.

Underline and Italics

Underline (or italicize) the titles of long works: books, magazines, newspapers, movies, plays, television series, and record albums. (Remember, though, that titles of short works are placed in quotation marks. See page 116.)

> Students in the current events class must skim <u>USA Today</u> every morning, read both <u>Time</u> and <u>Newsweek</u>, and watch <u>60 Minutes</u> and <u>Meet the Press</u>.

Note   Printed material uses *italics* instead of underlining. Also, if you are writing on a computer, use italics instead of underlining.

Practice

Insert semicolons, hyphens, dashes, parentheses, or underlines where needed in each of the following sentences.

1. The shipping weight of the computer is thirty nine pounds.

2. A jar of mustard, a bottle of beer, and half a can of cat food these were the contents of the refrigerator.

3. The latest issue of Reader's Digest includes some interesting articles: "The Town That Wouldn't Die," the story of a Texas suburb that survived an epidemic "Work Out at Work," a guide to starting an exercise club at the office and "Fatal Distraction," a first-person account of one man's battle against television addiction.

4. A new couple's budget should cover items such as 1 rent or mortgage, 2 food, 3 car expenses, 4 clothing, 5 entertainment, and, of course, 6 miscellaneous.

5. The most frightening book I ever read was Stephen King's The Tommy-knockers, and the most frightening movie I ever saw was The Fly.

32 More about Capital Letters

Other Rules for Capital Letters

1 Capitalize the names of geographic locations.

The **S**outhwest is known for its hot, dry climate, while **N**ew **E**ngland is famous for cold winters.

People from the **S**outh have a reputation for hospitality.

Note   Do not, however, capitalize words that mean directions (not places).

The mountains are **s**outh and slightly **w**est of here.

Drive six blocks **e**ast on Walnut Street and then turn **n**orth onto 23d Street.

2 Capitalize the names of historical periods and well-known events.

The **R**enaissance is a period famous for the art it produced.

The **M**y **L**ai **M**assacre was one of the ugliest incidents of the **V**ietnam **W**ar.

3 Capitalize all words in the opening of a letter and the first word in the closing.

Dear **P**rofessor **C**ross: **D**ear **M**s. **H**ill: **V**ery truly yours,   **W**ith all my love,

4 Capitalize common abbreviations made up of the first letters of the words they represent.

FBI   NAACP   NASA   IBM   NBC   UFO   AIDS

Note   Periods are usually not used in these abbreviations.

Practice

Capitalize words as necessary in the following sentences.

1. After serving in the korean war, my grandfather worked for the cia.

2. Although we've lived in the northeast for fifteen years, our neighbors do not consider us natives because we were born in the midwest.

3. The aids epidemic is often compared to a plague that killed millions during the period known as the dark ages.

4. On our pbs channel, we saw a nature program about the animals of Tanzania, a country located just south of Kenya.

5. dear sir or madam:

   Please have your store send me a replacement for the defective dvd player I bought from you last week.

   yours truly,

   Wanda Stern

33 More about Homonyms

Other Homonyms

all ready *completely prepared*
already *previously* or *before*

> Those cans of tuna have **already** been stacked too high; they appear **all ready** to fall on an unlucky shopper.

coarse (1) *rough;* (2) *crass* or *rude*
course (1) *a unit of instruction;* (2) *a part of a meal;* (3) *certainly* (with *of,* as in *of course*)

> The telephone operators are required to take a **course** in phone etiquette to ensure that they do not treat even irritating customers in a **coarse** manner.

lead *a metal*
led (past tense of *lead*) (1) *influenced* or *persuaded;* (2) *guided*

> The children's poor health **led** the doctor to suspect they were being poisoned by **lead**-based paint in their home.

pair *a set of two*
pear *a fruit*

> The **pear** tree in the backyard is home this spring to a **pair** of nesting doves.

principal (1) *main;* (2) *the person in charge of a school*
principle *a guideline* or *rule*

> The **principal** lectured incoming students about drugs. "Our **principle** is a simple one: if you bring drugs to school, you're out of school," she said.

Hint A trick to remembering one meaning of *principal* is that, ideally, a principal should be a **pal**—the last three letters in the word.

Other Confusing Words

Here are more words that people often have trouble telling apart.

a *one*—used before a consonant
an *one*—used before a vowel sound (*a, e, i, o, u,* or silent *h*)

a book	**a d**egree	**a m**istake	**a s**urprise	**a y**ard	**a h**ero
an assignment	**an e**gg	**an i**nstructor	**an o**range	**an u**ncle	**an h**onor

Note   The *h* in *hero* is pronounced, but the *h* in *honor* is silent. (The word *honor* is pronounced "ON-er.") Since *honor* begins with a vowel sound, *an* is correct.

accept   (1) *to receive (willingly); (2) to agree to*
except   (1) *to leave out;* (2) *but*

All the workers **except** the part-timers voted to **accept** the new contract.

advice   (rhymes with *nice*) *a suggestion* or *suggestions*
advise   (rhymes with *size*) *to give advice or suggestions to*

Most fortune-tellers' **advice** is pretty worthless; fortune-tellers **advise** their clients to become more and more dependent on them for guidance.

affect   *to influence* or *to have an effect on*
effect   (1) *to cause;* (2) *a result*

The heavy rain the night before did not **affect** the success of the picnic; in fact, the rain had the **effect** of clearing the air and producing a beautiful day.

among   used with three or more
between   used with two

A contest **among** eight candidates who campaigned for the presidency finally came down to a choice **between** two persons—a man and a woman.

desert   (pronounced DEZ-ert) *a dry and sandy place*
desert   (pronounced de-ZERT) *to leave behind*
dessert   (also pronounced de-ZERT) *the final course of a meal*

Lost in the wasteland of the **desert**, the stranded man dreamed of gallons of ice water and of a cool, refreshing **dessert**, such as orange sherbet.

does   (rhymes with *fuzz*) present tense of *do*
dose   (rhymes with *gross*) *a measured amount of medicine*

Does a double **dose** of cold medicine cure a cold twice as fast?

fewer   *smaller in number*—used with plurals (more than one thing)
less   *smaller in degree, value, or amount*—used with singular words (one thing)

If you work **fewer** hours, you will earn **less** money.

loose   (rhymes with *juice*) (1) *not tight;* (2) *free* or *not confined*
lose   (rhymes with *blues*) (1) *to misplace;* (2) *to get rid of*

It's easy to **lose** a ring that is too **loose** on one's finger.

Hint   Here's one way to remember which is which: *Loose* and *tight* both have five letters; *lose* and *find* both have four letters.

quiet   *silent*
quit   (1) *to give up;* (2) *to stop doing something*
quite   *very*

"This house is **quite** noisy," said the babysitter to the children. "If you don't become **quiet** soon, I'm going to **quit** being so patient."

were   (rhymes with *fur*) past tense of *are*
where   (rhymes with *air*) *in what place* or *to what place* (see page 146)

Where did the movie director get all the thousands of people who **were** hired for that immense crowd scene?

Practice

Underline the correct word or words in each group in parentheses.

1. The cocky young man had (all ready, already) decided to (quit, quite, quiet) school, and he refused to (accept, except) his family's (advise, advice) to reconsider.

2. The rich (desert, dessert) had the (effect, affect) of giving several guests a stomachache, so their host gave them each a (does, dose) of Pepto-Bismol.

3. If I'm going to (lose, loose) ten pounds, I'll just have to eat (fewer, less) fattening food, but it'll be worth it for (a, an) opportunity to wear the (pair, pear) of size ten designer jeans that's been hanging in my closet for (a, an) year.

4. To protect themselves from heat and sand, people who live in the (desert, dessert) wear (loose, lose) robes made of (coarse, course) material.

5. I was (all ready, already) to put my groceries on the counter when I saw the sign reading "Ten Items or (Fewer, Less)."

6. "It's (quiet, quit, quite) difficult to (quiet, quit, quite) smoking," the doctor said, "but I (advice, advise) you to give up cigarettes at once—smoking will (affect, effect) your life span."

7. "Please don't (desert, dessert) me," Kim begged her brother. "I don't know anyone at this party (accept, except) you."

8. In her American Government (coarse, course), Sarita is learning the (principal, principle) of the balance of power—how decision-making is divided (among, between) the three branches of the federal government.

9. Jameer walked up to the desk and said in a (quiet, quit, quite) voice, "What time (does, dose) the library close?"

10. The parents couldn't remember (were, where) the Christmas decorations (were, where) stored until their six-year-old (lead, led) them to the Christmas box stacked (among, between) many other boxes in the attic.

34 More about Word Choice

Inflated Words

Keep your writing simple. Overly fancy words may confuse (or unintentionally amuse) a reader. Look at the following example:

> The outdoor repast was deferred because of precipitation.

The sentence would communicate more effectively if it were written like this:

> The picnic was postponed because of rain.

Here are a few other inflated words and simple replacements for them:

Inflated	Simple	Inflated	Simple
ascertain	learn, find out	facilitate	help
assert	say	finalize, culminate	finish
commence	begin	inquire	ask
commend	praise	manifest	show
compensate	pay	parameters	limits
elucidate	explain	prior to	before
embark upon	begin	replenish	refill
endeavor	try	subsequent to	after

Practice

Cross out the two inflated expressions in each of the sentences below. Then rewrite the faulty expressions on the lines provided, using simpler language. Feel free to consult a dictionary to find the meanings of any of the inflated words.

1. Students must remit 50 percent of their tuition prior to the first day of classes.

   _____   _____

2. Nobody had ascertained when the next bus would depart.

   _____   _____

3. Working conditions in that store are good, but the remuneration is insufficient.

   _____   _____

4. Since the children were being vociferous, the babysitter endeavored to quiet them.

   _____   _____

5. Subsequent to the heavy rains, people piled sandbags to keep the river from inundating the nearby city.

   _____   _____

6. As soon as the game commenced, it was clear that the home team would be victorious.

   _____   _____

7. "I simply cannot believe any more of your justifications," Marva told Rodney. "You've prevaricated entirely too often."

   _____   _____

8. At a fine restaurant, someone will replenish your glass of water as soon as you deplete it.

   _____   _____

9. "As soon as you return to your domicile," my father said, "please transmit word that you arrived safely."

   _____   _____

10. On Thanksgiving, everyone in my family enjoys a delectable repast at Cousin Miriam's house.

    _____   _____

Part Three

Applying the Skills

Preview

Part Three contains twelve combined mastery tests and ten editing tests:

Name _____ Section _____ Date _____

VERBS

■ Combined Mastery Test 1

Each sentence contains a mistake involving (1) standard English or irregular verb forms, (2) subject-verb agreement, or (3) consistent verb tense. Cross out the incorrect verb, and write the correct form in the space provided.

_____ 1. Each of the sisters in that family have a tattoo.

_____ 2. The artist picked up a brush, stared hard at the model, and begins to paint.

_____ 3. To everyone's surprise, the newest member of the track team breaked the school record for the five-hundred-yard dash.

_____ 4. Because so many uninvited people came to the party, we runned out of food.

_____ 5. Three enormous bags of money was sitting in the trunk of the arrested man's car.

_____ 6. On Saturdays, Jeremy mows the grass, raked the leaves, and pulls the weeds.

_____ 7. Just as she was thinking about buying new shoes, Tanya sees a "Sale" sign in the shoe-store window.

_____ 8. Sleeping on the sunny windowsill is two black-and-white cats.

_____ 9. When George first met Lana, he thinks she was the most beautiful girl in the world.

_____ 10. I went to my favorite pizza parlor, where I ran into my ex-boyfriend, who pretends he didn't see me.

Name _____   Section _____   Date _____

Score: (Number right) _____ × 10 = _____%

VERBS

■ Combined Mastery Test 2

Each sentence contains a mistake involving (1) standard English or irregular verb forms, (2) subject-verb agreement, or (3) consistent verb tense. Cross out the incorrect verb, and write the correct form in the space provided.

_____   1. Although Charlene be teasing you, she doesn't mean to hurt your feelings.

_____   2. Several trees in our backyard needs to be cut down.

_____   3. At the first game of our baseball team's season, the oldest man in town throwed the opening pitch.

_____   4. Yvonne opened the refrigerator door, looked hungrily at the chocolate pudding inside, and closes the door again.

_____   5. The chickens roosting in the hen house squawks loudly every morning and evening.

_____   6. The sign said "Beware of the Dog," but the dog laying under the sign did not look very fierce.

_____   7. Is there any bagels left for breakfast?

_____   8. At the party Donny flirted with all the girls, tells all his best jokes, and danced up a storm.

_____   9. I was amazed when my friends described how far they had rode on their bicycles.

_____   10. My little cousin is only eleven, but she already play the piano better than I ever will.

Name _____   Section _____   Date _____

Score: (Number right) _____ × 10 = _____%

FRAGMENTS, RUN-ONS, AND COMMA SPLICES

■ Combined Mastery Test 3

In the space provided, indicate whether each item below contains a fragment (F), a run-on (R-O), or a comma splice (CS). Then correct the error.

_____ 1. The little boy liked his new glasses he thought they made him look grown-up. He wanted to wear them all the time, even while he slept.

_____ 2. Forest fires destroy thousands of acres of woodland every year. Many of them are started through acts of carelessness. Such as tossing a cigarette onto dry leaves.

_____ 3. Snow piled up in great drifts outside the door. Making it impossible to open. The family actually had to leave the house through a window.

_____ 4. A terrifying scream pierced the night, the friends screamed too and hugged each other. They all agreed it was the best haunted house they'd ever been to.

_____ 5. Matthew had never been called for jury duty before. He was very nervous as the trial started. But found the process fascinating.

_____ 6. The king's daughter stared in horror at the slimy green frog. How could she ever bring herself to kiss it? Even if it was an enchanted prince.

_____ 7. The juice of the aloe plant is very soothing, it can help heal burns and scrapes. Just break open a piece of the plant and rub the cool juice across your skin.

_____ 8. How can you eat that chili? It is so hot it made my eyes water I couldn't eat more than a spoonful.

_____ 9. Christmas comes earlier each year. Because merchants like to stretch out the buying season. Right after Halloween this year, store owners hung colored lights and filled their windows with Christmas decorations.

_____ 10. Darlene walked into the living room. She sat down next to her boyfriend, she held his hand. Then she gently said, "I can't marry you."

Name _____   Section _____   Date _____

Score: (Number right) _____ × 10 = _____%

FRAGMENTS, RUN-ONS, AND COMMA SPLICES

■ Combined Mastery Test 4

In the space provided, indicate whether each item below contains a fragment (F), a run-on (R-O), or a comma splice (CS). Then correct the error.

_____ 1. My mother insists that I look good wearing light yellow clothes. I think when I wear yellow, I look as though I had died. Several days ago.

_____ 2. As darkness began to fall, the searchers grew more anxious, they called the missing child's name again and again. To their great relief, they finally heard the child answer them.

_____ 3. Americans spend millions of dollars each year on bottled water, critics say that tap water is just as good. There are no plastic bottles to dispose of, and tap water is equally safe to drink.

_____ 4. When scientists found ancient seashells buried high on the mountain, they became very excited. They realized that the mountain had been below sea level. Many years ago.

_____ 5. Mrs. Morris gazed at her lazy son. Asleep on the couch for the fourth afternoon in a row. She decided the time had come for him to get a job.

_____ 6. I don't understand why you won't answer the telephone you're sitting closer to it than I am. Am I the only one who hears it?

_____ 7. *Gone with the Wind* was Vivica's favorite book when she was younger. For a few months, she even began speaking with a Southern accent. In imitation of Scarlett O'Hara.

_____ 8. For years, there have been reports of a strange manlike creature living in northern climates. The creature, whose existence has never been proved, has various names. Such as the Yeti, the Sasquatch, and the Abominable Snowman.

_____ 9. Garlic may smell bad it tastes delicious. It has other good qualities as well. Garlic helps lower cholesterol and is also supposed to keep vampires away.

_____ 10. There are no clocks in Las Vegas gambling casinos. If gamblers don't know what time it is. They'll stay longer and lose more money.

Name _____ Section _____ Date _____

Score: (Number right) _____ × 10 = _____ %

PRONOUNS

■ Combined Mastery Test 5

Each sentence contains a mistake involving (1) pronoun agreement, (2) pronoun reference, (3) pronoun point of view, or (4) pronoun form. Cross out each incorrect pronoun, and write the correction in the space provided.

_____ 1. If I have an "A" average, does that mean that you don't have to take the final exam?

_____ 2. Each of the football players had the team's name printed on the back of their jersey.

_____ 3. The police officer told Omar that he would get a fine for parking in a handi-capped space.

_____ 4. Between you and I, that restaurant does not serve food fit for humans.

_____ 5. If them seats aren't taken, could we sit there?

_____ 6. We wanted to order a hot meal after 10 P.M., but they said the kitchen was closed.

_____ 7. Our instructor was disappointed when nobody in the class volunteered to read their paper out loud.

_____ 8. I don't like the new movies even though every reviewer has praised it.

_____ 9. When our union called for a strike, all of us had to stay home from work, even if they didn't want to.

_____ 10. If anyone is going to the convenience store, would they bring me a bag of potato chips?

Name _____   Section _____   Date _____

Score: (Number right) _____ × 10 = _____%

PRONOUNS

■ Combined Mastery Test 6

Each sentence contains a mistake involving (1) pronoun agreement, (2) pronoun reference, (3) pronoun point of view, or (4) pronoun form. Cross out each incorrect pronoun, and write the correction in the space provided.

_____   1. Neither of my brothers likes their job.

_____   2. Heather and me are having a contest to see who can lose more weight.

_____   3. Last night, Elena hung her new dress in the closet, and now she can't find it.

_____   4. If we can't find our voter registration card, will you be stopped from voting?

_____   5. This here microwave must be broken—all it does is buzz.

_____   6. When my neighbors bought new tires, they were very cheap.

_____   7. I like eating at that restaurant because the servers always bring you free refills for drinks.

_____   8. Both of my sisters get her hair done at the same salon.

_____   9. One of the classroom buildings is having their roof repaired.

_____   10. Nearly every day, several people call my home office, wanting me to participate in a survey or offering a free vacation. I wish this would stop so I could get some work done!

Name _____ Section _____ Date _____

Score: (Number right) _____ × 10 = _____ %

CAPITAL LETTERS AND PUNCTUATION

■ Combined Mastery Test 7

Each of the following sentences contains an error in capitalization or punctuation. Refer to the box below and, in the space provided, write the letter identifying the error. Then correct the error.

a.	missing capital letter
b.	missing apostrophe
c.	missing quotation marks
d.	missing comma

_____ 1. During my haircut, it made me very nervous to hear my barber say, Oops.

_____ 2. Most of the towns citizens agree that the mayor is doing a fine job.

_____ 3. My math class is not too difficult, but my english class is driving me crazy.

_____ 4. "Please close your books and put away your notes" said Mrs. Shoup. "It is time for a quiz."

_____ 5. If you know you cant keep a secret, you should warn your friends not to tell you any.

_____ 6. Everyone knows that my uncles hair isn't real, but we all pretend to think it is.

_____ 7. "I tell you, my whole life has been tough," said the comedian. When I was a kid, I had to tie a pork chop around my neck so the dog would play with me."

_____ 8. Even though we told him the four o'clock party began at three o'clock my brother still showed up two hours late.

_____ 9. If you drive forty miles north of here, you will reach the michigan line.

_____ 10. *Rebecca,* a wonderful novel by Daphne du Maurier is about a woman who is haunted by her husband's former wife.

Name _____   Section _____   Date _____

Score: (Number right) _____ × 10 = _____%

CAPITAL LETTERS AND PUNCTUATION

■ Combined Mastery Test 8

Each of the following sentences contains an error in capitalization or punctuation. Refer to the box below and, in the space provided, write the letter identifying the error. Then correct the error.

a.	missing capital letter
b.	missing apostrophe
c.	missing quotation marks
d.	missing comma

_____   1. If youve got time before school, would you take the trash out to the curb?

_____   2. Almost nine hundred people showed up to audition for a part in the movie but only two were chosen.

_____   3. My mother always insisted on using crisco shortening in her pie crust, but I use any brand I happen to have on hand.

_____   4. "On my first date with your mother, my father told me, "her little brother came along to make sure I behaved myself."

_____   5. A real banana split should contain a banana three scoops of ice cream, whipped cream, peanuts, and a cherry.

_____   6. As I carefully eased open the front door, I heard my mother's stern voice say, "you missed your curfew."

_____   7. For the Bradshaw family, it's a tradition to watch the movie It's a wonderful Life at least once during the holiday season.

_____   8. Although Jimmy claims to hate tomatoes he loves spaghetti sauce and pizza.

_____   9. My sisters boyfriend gave her a ring that quickly turned her finger green.

_____   10. "I'm giving you three weeks to work on this project," announced Mrs. Smithfield, so I don't expect anyone to ask for extra time."

Name _____ Section _____ Date _____

Score: (Number right) _____ × 5 = _____%

HOMONYMS AND WORD CHOICE

■ Combined Mastery Test 9

Each of the following groups of sentences contains two errors. The errors involve either homonym mistakes or ineffective word choices: slang, clichés, or wordy expressions. Underline the two errors. Then write the corrections in the spaces provided.

_____

_____

1. Why do I have to take algebra? I couldn't care less about it. In addition, I don't see how a math course will lead me too a decent job.

_____

_____

2. At the county fair, we saw the fattest pig in size you can imagine. We also walked threw a barn where cows were being milked.

_____

_____

3. Wear my sister is going, the weather will be warm, so she is packing light. She is taking just two pears of shorts, two T-shirts, and a sweatshirt.

_____

_____

4. Brad eagerly excepted his aunt's offer of a summer job. He knew he'd really lucked out to get it, and he was determined to make the most of it.

_____

_____

5. Although Maria and Teresa are the best of friends, there personalities are very different. Maria is quite and shy, while Teresa is talkative and outgoing.

_____

_____

6. I am constantly loosing my house key. I guess I'm just to absentminded. Maybe I should tie it on a string around my neck.

_____

_____

7. Is the knew movie "one of the most exciting ever made" or "a waste of two hours"? It depends on weather you believe one critic or another.

_____

_____

8. The girl that Paul is beginning to date seems to really like him. She has all ready invited him to hang out with her family at Thanksgiving.

_____

_____

9. I can't believe that you spent fifteen dollars to have you're fortune told. If you ask me, a fortune-teller's advise is just a waste of money.

_____

_____

10. "I worked my fingers to the bone preparing the desert for tonight's dinner," Hannah laughingly told her guests. "I had to drive all the way to the bakery and all the way back again."

Name _____ Section _____ Date _____

Score: (Number right) _____ × 5 = _____%

HOMONYMS AND WORD CHOICE

■ ## Combined Mastery Test 10

Each of the following groups of sentences contains two errors. The errors involve either homonym mistakes or ineffective word choices: slang, clichés, or wordy expressions. Underline the two errors. Then write the corrections in the spaces provided.

_____
_____

1. If its sunny tomorrow, we are going to go for a long bike ride. But if the whether is bad, we're going to rent videos and watch them all day.

_____
_____

2. Nobody knows what the man next door dose for a living. He never seems to go to work, but he has the best wheels in the neighborhood.

_____
_____

3. At the school's annual costume party, everyone was amazed too see the most serious teacher of them all arrive. He hopped into the room, dressed as a huge rabbit that was pink in color.

_____
_____

4. Although many children believe in Santa Claus, it's quiet unusual to find an adult who thinks Santa is real. My sister's boyfriend, however, is an unusual dude.

_____
_____

5. Larry thinks the secret of happiness is being rich. Coming into the possession of money is more important to him then anything else in the world.

_____
_____

6. Sarah looked as pretty as a picture at the awards banquet. She was wearing a very plane black dress, but she'd dressed it up with a new silver necklace and earrings.

_____
_____

7. Don't you hate it when someone says, "Oh, I don't want dessert," but then wants a peace of whatever you order? In my opinion, their just being rude in doing that.

_____
_____

8. Our star player sprained his ankle, but fortunately, he didn't brake it. We need him back in the lineup soon, or we'll have know chance in the playoffs.

_____
_____

9. The Taylors are to protective of there children. They won't let them ride bicycles, play softball, or roller-skate, believing that they're going to get badly hurt.

_____
_____

10. Didn't anyone else here that loud party going on last night? I was already to call the police when it finally quieted down at 3 A.M.

Name _____ Section _____ Date _____

Score: (Number right) _____ × 10 = _____ %

FAULTY MODIFIERS AND PARALLELISM

■ Combined Mastery Test 11

In the spaces at the left, indicate whether each sentence contains a misplaced modifier (MM), a dangling modifier (DM), or faulty parallelism (FP). Then correct the errors in the space between the lines.

_____ 1. Forgetting that it was due, my English paper was turned in late.

_____ 2. My father always said coffee should be strong as sin, sweet as love, and it should be as hot as blazes.

_____ 3. Making a loud grating sound, Michelle stopped the car to see what was wrong.

_____ 4. Bob noticed a police officer driving behind him with a sense of dread.

_____ 5. Hitting the "snooze" button on my alarm clock, my eyes just wouldn't open.

_____ 6. Playing cards, to watch football, and working in the garden are my grandfather's favorite activities.

_____ 7. While trying on an old pair of blue jeans, Marvin's waistband wouldn't close.

_____ 8. Gina uses her computer to send e-mail, get school papers written, and search the Internet.

_____ 9. "Don't you feel well? You're hardly eating anything!" June said to her teenage son.

_____ 10. I couldn't find my car keys, even though I searched in my coat pockets, on the kitchen shelf, and looked inside every drawer in the house.

Name _____   Section _____   Date _____

Score: (Number right) _____ × 10 = _____ %

FAULTY MODIFIERS AND PARALLELISM

■ Combined Mastery Test 12

In the spaces at the left, indicate whether each sentence contains a misplaced modifier (MM), a dangling modifier (DM), or faulty parallelism (FP). Then correct the errors in the space between the lines.

_____ 1. Cleaning the bathroom, doing the laundry, and to scrub the kitchen floor are among my least favorite chores.

_____ 2. Glaring angrily at each other, it was easy to tell that Ron and Helen's argument was serious.

_____ 3. The little boy stared in wonder at the elephant sitting on his father's shoulders.

_____ 4. Bending almost double in the strong wind, I was surprised the trees didn't break.

_____ 5. Without a word of good-bye, the car sped off with Teron at the wheel.

_____ 6. High fever, a hacking cough, and muscles that ache are all symptoms of the flu.

_____ 7. Denzel almost received fifty e-mails yesterday.

_____ 8. In my dreams, I am often a star athlete, a scientist who is brilliant, or a talented rock musician.

_____ 9. We enjoyed the delicious barbecue that our neighbors had prepared with hearty appetites.

_____ 10. Clicking all the buttons on the remote control, my search for something good to watch on TV was unsuccessful.

Name _____ Section _____ Date _____

Score: (Number right) _____ × 20 = _____ %

EDITING TEST 1

Identify the sentence-skills mistakes at the underlined spots in the selection that follows. From the box below, choose the letter that describes each mistake and write it in the space provided. Then, in the spaces between the lines, correct each mistake.

a.	comma splice
b.	fragment
c.	missing capital letter
d.	missing apostrophe
e.	missing comma

Every year, on the third Sunday in May, the world's largest footrace is held, it takes
                                                                                    1
place in San Francisco, California. As many as 100,000 runners participate in the Bay
            1
to Breakers Run, a twelve-kilometer run that begins at the San Francisco Bay and ends

at the Pacific ocean. Although some of the worlds best runners participate in the race,
              2   3
many others are less serious about winning. Costumed runners dress up as almost anything

imaginable. Including human tacos, palm trees, and even the Golden Gate Bridge. Groups
            4
of thirteen runners tied together compete as human centipedes. Waiters jog along, trying

to balance glasses of champagne resting on trays. The race which has been held annually
                                                              5
since 1912, is as much fun to watch as it is to participate in.

1. _____   2. _____   3. _____   4. _____   5. _____

Name _____   Section _____   Date _____
Score: (Number right) _____ × 20 = _____%

EDITING TEST 2

Identify the sentence-skills mistakes at the underlined spots in the selection that follows. From the box below, choose the letter that describes each mistake and write it in the space provided. Then, in the spaces between the lines, correct each mistake.

a.	faulty parallelism
b.	inconsistent verb tense
c.	fragment
d.	run-on
e.	missing comma

If you know the name of Leonardo da Vinci, it is probably as an artist. Leonardo produced some of the world's most famous paintings, including the *Mona Lisa* and *The Last Supper*. But Leonardo was not only an artist. He also deserves to be known as an inventor, a scientist, <u>and he worked in engineering too</u>. Leonardo was born in 1452. He
1
<u>goes</u> to Florence, Italy, to study art when he was a teenager. Although he became an official
2
"court artist," he also found time to dream up dozens of inventions. <u>Some became realities</u>
3
<u>in his lifetime others were left for the future</u>. Among the many designs that Leonardo came
3
up with were those for flying machines, <u>parachutes submarines</u>, and underwater breathing
4
devices. Although he was a gentle vegetarian, Leonardo also designed many new weapons. By the time he died in 1519, Leonardo was recognized as a genius. <u>One of the greatest the</u>
5
<u>world had ever produced</u>.
5

1. _____   2. _____   3. _____   4. _____   5. _____

Name _____ Section _____ Date _____

Score: (Number right) _____ × 20 = _____ %

EDITING TEST 3

Identify the sentence-skills mistakes at the underlined spots in the selection that follows. From the box below, choose the letter that describes each mistake and write it in the space provided. Then, in the spaces between the lines, correct each mistake.

a.	fragment
b.	run-on
c.	inconsistent verb tense
d.	homonym mistake
e.	missing quotation mark

Recently something happened that made me feel like a human dinosaur. I was taking care of my eight-year-old niece for the afternoon. I said I wanted to talk to an old friend of mine who lives in another state. Kate <u>says</u>, "Why don't you e-mail her?" I answered, ₁ "Because I don't have a computer, and I don't know how to use e-mail, anyway." Kate stared at me. <u>As if I'd just said I didn't know how to tie my shoes.</u> <u>"How can anybody not</u> ₂   ₃ <u>know how to use e-mail?" she said she really didn't seem able to believe it.</u> The next week ₃ Kate came over to visit again. This time she had her friend Paige with her. "Paige wanted to meet you," she said. Feeling flattered, I said, "Well, hello, Paige." "Hi," Paige said. <u>I've</u> ₄ never met anyone who couldn't use e-mail before. My brother said you must be one of those people who lives in the <u>passed</u>." I gave them cookies and sent them home. I guess it ₅ could be worse. At least Kate didn't take me to school for show-and-tell.

1. _____   2. _____   3. _____   4. _____   5. _____

Name _____ Section _____ Date _____

Score: (Number right) _____ × 20 = _____%

EDITING TEST 4

Identify the sentence-skills mistakes at the underlined spots in the selection that follows. From the box below, choose the letter that describes each mistake and write it in the space provided. Then, in the spaces between the lines, correct each mistake.

a.	fragment
b.	comma splice
c.	inconsistent verb tense
d.	homonym mistake
e.	missing apostrophe

Do you have a memory that makes you burn with shame, even years after the event?

I do. A boy I didn't know very well had walked up to me in the lunchroom. And asked me
₁

for a date. I was so surprised that I automatically said yes. Later, though, I start to have
₁   ₂

second thoughts. I didnt think I would have any fun. I began to wish I had said no. And so,
₃

a few hours before our date, I called him. Trying to sound miserable, I said I was to sick to
₄

go out. He politely said that was all right. Feeling much better, I instantly called a girlfriend

and arranged to go out for pizza. When we arrived, there in the pizza parlor was the boy

I had stood up. I'll never forget the disappointed look he gave me. Over the next few years,

I realized that he was a really great guy and that I'd been an idiot not to go out with him.

But by then, of course, I'd lost my chance, he never spoke to me again.
₅

1. _____   2. _____   3. _____   4. _____   5. _____

Name _____ Section _____ Date _____

Score: (Number right) _____ × 20 = _____%

EDITING TEST 5

Identify the sentence-skills mistakes at the underlined spots in the selection that follows. From the box below, choose the letter that describes each mistake and write it in the space provided. Then, in the spaces between the lines, correct each mistake.

> a. missing capital letter
> b. faulty parallelism
> c. homonym mistake
> d. comma splice
> e. fragment

My great-aunt was an unusual woman, she liked animals at least as much as she
                                     1
liked humans. She lived in a house with a big backyard that faced a forest. Over the years,
      1
she took in dozens of wounded or orphaned animals. Visitors never new what they would
                                                                 2
find when they stopped by her house. I remember seeing broken-legged blue jays, bullet-
wounded squirrels, and owls with one eye living there. She once raised a family of baby
                        3
foxes, feeding them from a bottle. And then returned them to the woods. When my aunt
                                    4
died, she left the little bit of money she had to the Society for the prevention of Cruelty to
                                                                     5
Animals.

1. _____   2. _____   3. _____   4. _____   5. _____

Name _____ Section _____ Date _____

Score: (Number right) _____ × 10 = _____%

EDITING TEST 6

Identify the sentence-skills mistakes at the underlined spots in the selection that follows. From the box below, choose the letter that describes each mistake and write it in the space provided. Then, in the spaces between the lines, correct each mistake. (The number in parentheses indicates how many of each mistake occur in the selection.)

> a. fragment (2)
> b. pronoun mistake (2)
> c. apostrophe mistake (2)
> d. homonym mistake (1)
> e. mistake in subject-verb agreement (1)
> f. missing quotation mark (1)
> g. unnecessary comma (1)

Many of us are annoyed by telemarketer's who call you day and night, trying to sell
                                 1   2
everything from magazine subscriptions, to vacation homes. These electronic intruders
                                        3
dont seem to care how much they are inconveniencing us. And refuse to take "no" for an
4   5
answer. However, nuisance callers can be stopped if we take charge of the conversation.
5
As soon as one of them asks how we are doing. We should respond, "Fine, and are you
                                          6
a telephone solicitor? This technique puts the caller on the defensive. We then have an
                7
opening to say that we do not accept solicitations over the phone, only threw the mail. This
                                                                      8   9
puts a quick end to the conversation. Of course, anyone who prefer not to be called at all
                                                            10
can sign up at the National Do Not Call Registry at **www.donotcall.gov** and be safe from

annoying calls for five years.

1. _____   2. _____   3. _____   4. _____   5. _____

6. _____   7. _____   8. _____   9. _____   10. _____

Name _____ Section _____ Date _____

Score: (Number right) _____ × 10 = _____%

EDITING TEST 7

Identify the sentence-skills mistakes at the underlined spots in the selection that follows. From the box below, choose the letter that describes each mistake and write it in the space provided. Then, in the spaces between the lines, correct each mistake. (The number in parentheses indicates how many of each mistake occur in the selection.)

a. fragment (2)
b. run-on (1)
c. missing comma (2)
d. homonym mistake (2)
e. mistake in subject-verb agreement (1)
f. dangling modifier (1)
g. comma splice (1)

Millions of people in this country is terrified of going to the dentist. If you are one
<u>1</u>

of them, you should know that some dentists specialize in treating people. Who are very
<u>2</u>

fearful of dental work. These dentists encourage patients to discuss there fears and will
<u>2</u>   <u>3</u>

answer questions in an honest, understanding manner. Even if your dentist does not have

such a specialty you can arrange to use a signal such as raising your right hand, if you
<u>4</u>   <u>5</u>

experience too much pain. This will give you a feeling of control it will also guarantee that
<u>6</u>

the pain—if any—will not go beyond what you can tolerate. You can also try a relaxation
<u>6</u>

technique. Breathing deeply before and during appointments, your fears will subside. A
<u>7</u>   <u>8</u>

last good idea is to bring an iPod, you can then listen to your favorite music in the dental
<u>8</u>

chair. Its hard for the brain to register pain. When your favorite song is filling your head.
<u>8</u> <u>9</u>   <u>10</u>

1. _____   2. _____   3. _____   4. _____   5. _____

6. _____   7. _____   8. _____   9. _____   10. _____

Name _____   Section _____   Date _____

Score: (Number right) _____ × 10 = _____%

EDITING TEST 8

Identify the sentence-skills mistakes at the underlined spots in the selection that follows. From the box below, choose the letter that describes each mistake and write it in the space provided. Then, in the spaces between the lines, correct each mistake.

a.	fragment	f.	pronoun mistake
b.	comma splice	g.	missing comma
c.	irregular verb mistake	h.	missing apostrophe
d.	mistake in subject-verb agreement	i.	missing quotation mark
e.	inconsistent verb tense	j.	misplaced modifier

When President Theodore "Teddy" Roosevelt visited the South in 1902. He was
                                                              1
invited to a hunting party. The organizers of the hunt was eager for the President to have a
                                                       2
successful hunt. They tied a bear cub to a stake so that the President could not miss it. After
                                                                                         3
he realized that the bear could not escape Roosevelt refused to fire. A political cartoon was
                                            4
printed in a number of newspapers based on the incident. The cartoon, with a drawing of
                                  5
the small bear, was seen by a shop owner in Brooklyn. The shop owner then maked up a
                                                                                6
window display version of the little bear in a soft plush material. Before offering the bear
to customers, the shop owner asks Roosevelt for permission to sell the new toy as "Teddys
                                7   8
Bear." The President gave his approval but wrote, I don't think my name is worth much to
                                                9
the toy bear cub business." He was clearly wrong, a bear-buying frenzy swept the country.
                                                                10
The teddy bear has been popular ever since.

1. _____   2. _____   3. _____   4. _____   5. _____

6. _____   7. _____   8. _____   9. _____   10. _____

Name _____ Section _____ Date _____

Score: (Number right) _____ × 10 = _____%

EDITING TEST 9

See if you can locate and correct the ten sentence-skills mistakes in the selection that follows. The mistakes are listed in the box below. As you locate each mistake, write the number of the word group containing it in the space provided. Then, in the spaces between the lines, correct each mistake.

1 fragment _____	2 homonym mistakes _____
1 run-on _____	_____
1 missing comma _____	1 misplaced modifier _____
1 unnecessary comma _____	1 dangling modifier _____
1 apostrophe mistake _____	1 faulty parallelism _____

[1]Some people believe the superstition that cats have nine lives because they can fall with few, if any, injuries from high places. [2]They may have minor injuries, such as a bloody nose or cracked teeth or ribs but they recover. [3]Cats are able to survive long falls because they possess several advantages. [4]For one thing, there small size and body weight that is low soften the impact. [5]As they make contact with the ground. [6]Also, cats have highly developed inner ears these give them a keen sense of balance. [7]Quickly adjusting themselves in the air and landing on all four feet, the impact is absorbed by their legs. [8]Additionally, cats bend their legs when they land. [9]This cushions and spreads the impact, not only through bones that might brake otherwise, but through a cats joints, and muscles as well.

Name _____ Section _____ Date _____

Score: (Number right) _____ × 10 = _____%

EDITING TEST 10

See if you can locate and correct the ten sentence-skills mistakes in the selection that follows. The mistakes are listed in the box below. As you locate each mistake, write the number of the word group containing it in the space provided. Then, in the spaces between the lines, correct each mistake.

1 fragment _____	1 missing comma _____
1 run-on _____	1 missing quotation mark _____
1 inconsistent verb tense _____	1 missing hyphen _____
1 mistake in subject-verb agreement _____	1 homonym mistake _____
1 missing capital letter _____	1 faulty parallelism _____

¹One of the top April fool's Day hoaxes of all time was created by Burger King. ²On April 1, a few years ago, Burger King placed a full-page advertisement in *USA Today*. ³The ad stated that an item were being added to their menu it was a "Left-Handed Whopper" specially designed for the 32,000,000 left-handed Americans. ⁴The knew sandwich included the same ingredients as the original Whopper (lettuce tomato, a patty made of hamburger, etc.), but all the condiments are rotated 180 degrees for the benefit of their left-handed customers. ⁵Burger King issued a follow-up press release the next day. ⁶According to the press release, although the Left-Handed Whopper was a hoax, thousands of customers had gone into restaurants. ⁷To order the new sandwich. ⁸The release went on to add, "Many others requested their own right handed version.

Limited Answer Key

Important Note   To strengthen your grammar, punctuation, and usage skills, you must do more than simply find out which of your answers are right and which are wrong. You also need to figure out (with the help of this book, the teacher, or other students) *why* you missed the items you answered incorrectly. By using each of your wrong answers as a learning opportunity, you will strengthen your understanding of the skills. You will also prepare yourself for the chapter tests, for which answers are not given here.

ANSWERS TO THE PRACTICES IN THE INTRODUCTION

Practice 1 (p. 3)

Note   Answers will vary. Below are some possibilities.

1. package
2. Donovan
3. paper
4. tree
5. job

Practice 2 (p. 3)

1. hawk, tree, yard
2. end, game, teams
3. headline, Change, America
4. Cara, letters, ink
5. workers, jobs, hours

Practice 3 (p. 4)

1. She . . . it
2. They . . . her
3. I . . . your
4. He (*or* She) . . . them
5. him . . . his

Practice 4 (p. 6)

Note   Answers will vary. Below are some possibilities.

1. cut
2. sleeps
3. asked

4. mows
5. graded

Practice 5 (p. 7)

1. were
2. am
3. look
4. is
5. feel

Practice 6 (p. 7)

1. should
2. could
3. must
4. has been
5. does

Practice 7 (p. 8)

1. with
2. in
3. Without
4. of
5. by

Practice 8 (p. 9)

Note   Answers will vary. Below are some possibilities.

1. hungry . . . large
2. old . . . torn
3. dark . . . lonely

4. wilted . . . overripe
5. slight . . . sore

Practice 9 (p. 10)

Note   Answers will vary. Below are some possibilities.

1. quickly
2. carefully . . . slowly
3. softly
4. happily
5. rarely . . . very

Practice 10 (p. 11)

1. or
2. but
3. so
4. and

Practice 11 (p. 13)

1. when
2. Because
3. Even though
4. Before
5. until

Practice 12 (p. 13)

1. Either . . . or
2. both . . . and
3. neither . . . nor

ANSWERS TO THE PRACTICES IN PART ONE

1 SUBJECTS AND VERBS

Practice 1 (p. 19)

1. *Subject:* Nikki   *Verb:* waited
2. *Subject:* dog   *Verb:* padded
3. *Subject:* One   *Verb:* is
4. *Subject:* kittens   *Verb:* need
5. *Subject:* I   *Verb:* have

Practice 2 (p. 20)

1. *Subject:* Everyone
   Verb: is working
2. *Subject:* list
   Verb: will be posted
3. *Subject:* siren
   Verb: began
4. *Subject:* shirt
   Verb: should have been put
5. *Subject:* you
   Verb: must remember

2 MORE ABOUT VERBS

Practice 1 (p. 29)

1. began
2. broken
3. eaten, drank
4. driven, saw
5. read, written, taken

Practice 2 (p. 30)

1. dresses
2. dropped
3. looked
4. hate
5. manages

Practice 3 (p. 31)

1. did
2. has
3. were
4. doesn't
5. was

Practice 4 (p. 32)

1. realized
2. disappears

3. discovered
4. want
5. yelled

3 SUBJECT-VERB AGREEMENT

Practice 1 (p. 40)

1. *Subject:* workers
   Verb: like
2. *Subject:* women
   Verb: score
3. *Subject:* noise
   Verb: hurts
4. *Subject:* bag
   Verb: contains
5. *Subject:* instructions
   Verb: are

Practice 2 (p. 41)

1. *Subject:* keys
   Verb: are
2. *Subject:* hundreds
   Verb: live
3. *Subject:* people
   Verb: were
4. *Subject:* dogs
   Verb: do
5. *Subject:* boxes
   Verb: are

Practice 3 (p. 42)

1. *Subject:* Everything
   Verb: is
2. *Subject:* Neither
   Verb: works
3. *Subject:* No one
   Verb: is
4. *Subject:* Each
   Verb: deserves
5. *Subject:* Everybody
   Verb: knows

Practice 4 (p. 42)

1. *Subject:* cats, dog
   Verb: stay
2. *Subject:* CDs, DVDs
   Verb: Are
3. *Subject:* Staples, Scotch tape
   Verb: hold

4. *Subject:* scratches, dents
   Verb: were
5. *Subject:* course, course
   Verb: require

4 SENTENCE TYPES

Practice 1 (p. 50)

Note Answers will vary. Below are some possibilities.

1. library
2. threw
3. Roast beef . . . Swiss cheese
4. Sylvia . . . jog
5. My aunt . . . uncle . . . ate

Practice 2 (p. 51)

1. Rodrigo is usually cheerful, but he seems quiet and troubled today.
2. All my clothes were dirty this morning, so I'm wearing my husband's shirt.
3. Virginia has learned karate, and she carries a can of self-defense spray.

Practice 3 (p. 52)

1. As the familiar "Wedding March" played, the bride and her father walked down the aisle.
2. Jeff broke out in red blotches after he walked through a bank of poison ivy.
3. Although Mei Lin scrubbed for an hour, she could not get the crayon marks off the wall.

5 FRAGMENTS

Note Methods of correction may vary.

Practice 1 (p. 61)

1. <u>When the hometown baseball team won the World Series,</u> two million people showed up at the victory parade.

2. <u>Because smoke detectors are so important to a family's safety</u>, their batteries should be checked often.

3. <u>After the children washed the family car</u>, they had a water fight with the wet sponges.

4. Please hang up the damp towel <u>that you just threw on the floor</u>.

Practice 2 (p. 62)

1. Police officers stood near the corner. They were <u>directing people around the accident</u>.

2. The magician ran a sword through the box <u>to prove no one was hiding inside</u>.

3. <u>Sitting quietly on the couch</u>, the dog didn't look as if he'd eaten my sandwich.

4. The restaurant has introduced a new vegetarian menu. Its purpose is <u>to attract diners who prefer not to eat meat</u>.

Practice 3 (p. 63)

1. Television censors watch out for material that viewers might find offensive, <u>such as sexual or racial jokes</u>.

2. The children's toys were everywhere <u>except in the toy chest</u>.

3. All applicants at that company must take a skills assessment test. They must <u>also</u> take <u>a personality profile test</u>.

4. The film class saw every Dustin Hoffman film, <u>including his first one, *The Graduate*</u>.

Practice 4 (p. 64)

1. Our instructor seems strict <u>but is actually friendly and helpful</u>.

2. A mouse's face popped out of a hole near the sink. <u>Then it disappeared quickly</u>.

3. The nurse brought the patient an extra pillow and a glass of water. <u>But she forgot his pain medication</u>.

4. The pot of coffee sat on the burner for hours <u>and became too strong and bitter to drink</u>.

6 RUN-ONS AND COMMA SPLICES

Note   Methods of correction may vary.

Practice 1 (p. 73)

1. It's easy to begin smoking, but it's much harder to quit.

2. Because some people at the office have gotten raises, the other workers are jealous.

3. The patient's blood pressure was low. His temperature was low as well.

Practice 2 (p. 74)

1. Hakim was talking on the phone, and he was switching TV channels with his remote control at the same time.

2. I chose the shortest checkout line at the supermarket. Then the one customer in front of me pulled out dozens of coupons.

3. Since the electricity at Jasmin's house went out, she had to write her paper by candlelight.

7 PRONOUNS

Practice 1 (p. 83)

1. she
2. their
3. he or she
4. it
5. him

Practice 2 (p. 83)

1. his father
2. the maintenance people
3. the sugar
4. cheating
5. the stores

Practice 3 (p. 84)

1. I
2. his
3. They

4. we
5. you

8 COMMA

Practice 1 (p. 92)

1. newspapers, aluminum,
2. Walking, bicycling,
3. kids, loaded the van,
4. insomnia, inability to concentrate,

Practice 2 (p. 92)

1. course,
2. on,
3. doorway,
4. hours,

Practice 3 (p. 93)

1. Beatles, who originally called themselves the Quarrymen,
2. yogurt, a dessert that is relatively low in calories,
3. dieters, on the other hand,
4. building, forty stories high,

Practice 4 (p. 94)

1. help, but
2. glasses, so
3. quickly, but
4. family, and

Practice 5 (p. 94)

1. replied,
2. ends,"
3. women," the mall store owner bragged,
4. do,"

9 APOSTROPHE

Practice 1 (p. 102)

1. What's, that's
2. you'll, it's
3. I'd, who's
4. isn't, aren't
5. didn't, they're

Practice 2 (p. 103)

1. It's, its
2. their, they're
3. Who's, whose
4. your, your
5. It's, their, whose, your

Practice 3 (p. 104)

2. mail carrier's job, that man's vicious dog
3. Everyone's assignment, Monday's class
4. Ben Franklin's inventions, people's ideas
5. Doris's grades, her brothers' grades

Practice 4 (p. 105)

1. Lucy's
   messages—plural
2. storefront's
   years—plural
3. manager's
   gives—verb
   assignments—plural
4. year's
   shows—plural
   programs—plural
   seasons—plural
5. son's
   coughs—verb
   wheezes—verb
   starts—verb
6. Theo's
   failings—plural
   conclusions—plural
7. Dieters—plural
   glasses—plural
   water's
8. dozens—plural
   elephants—plural
   water holes'
   edges—plural

10   QUOTATION MARKS

Practice 1 (p. 114)

1. "My throat is so sore I can't talk,"
2. "Life's a tough proposition, and the first hundred years are the hardest."
3. "Don't go in that door!"
4. "Parking By Permit Only—Violators Will Be Towed."
5. "If at first you don't succeed," . . . "you should read the directions."

Practice 2 (p. 115)

2. Coach Hodges told Lori, "You played an outstanding game."
3. Manuel insisted, "My new glasses haven't improved my vision one bit."
4. The detective exclaimed, "I know the murderer's identity!"
5. I told Dr. Patton, "I haven't been to a dentist since high school."

Practice 3 (p. 116)

1. The Good Food Book . . . "How to Eat More and Weigh Less."
2. "The Garden Party."
3. The Sound of Music, . . . "Climb Every Mountain"
4. "All Gamblers Lose" . . . Newsweek . . . Time.
5. "Will the Circle Be Unbroken?" . . . The Atlantic Monthly

11   OTHER PUNCTUATION MARKS

Practice 1 (p. 124)

1. close?
2. aggressive.
3. birth!
4. run.
5. bins.

Practice 2 (p. 126)

1. black-hatted
2. (I think I've mentioned her to you before)
3. all—if
4. attachments:
5. diet;

12   CAPITAL LETTERS

Practice 1 (p. 135)

1. As, Doug, Don't
2. St. Mary's, Seminary, Baltimore, Maryland, Catholic
3. We, Professor, Henderson, Florentine, Italian, Lake, Street
4. Some, Rodeo, Drive, Beverly, Hills, California
5. When, Rodney, Dangerfield, I

Practice 2 (p. 136)

1. Caucasian, African-American, Hispanic, Asian
2. All, Shook, Up, Pepsi
3. Introduction, Statistics
4. Monday, October, Columbus, Day
5. Mommy, Solarcaine

13   HOMONYMS

Practice (p. 145)

1. It's, it's, its
2. There, their, they're
3. to, two, too
4. You're, you're, your

14   WORD CHOICE

Note   Wording of answers may vary.

Practice 1 (p. 155)

1. Because the judge's hair is prematurely gray, people think she is much older than thirty-eight.

2. The company is now taking many steps to reduce environmental pollution.

3. If the weather is bad, the baseball game will be postponed.

Practice 2 (p. 156)

1. do very well in . . . deliberately miss

2. was fortunate . . . fired

3. fell asleep . . . working all night

Practice 3 (p. 156)

1. very sick . . . healthy

2. there wasn't much time left . . . accept the situation

3. unexpectedly . . . traveled quickly

15 MISPLACED AND DANGLING MODIFIERS

Note Wording of answers may vary.

Practice 1 (p. 164)

1. With shaking hands, the young man gave his driver's license to the officer.

2. Driving down the country road, we were surprised to hear a siren.

3. Gina got badly sunburned on her face and back after spending a day at the beach.

4. The registrar will post on the Web site the schedule for final exams.

5. Stan bought a sports car with wire wheels from a fast-talking salesman.

Practice 2 (p. 165)

1. I studied for only ten minutes; then I took a nap.

2. Carlos must have answered almost a hundred ads before he found a job.

3. My sister spends nearly all evening on the telephone.

Practice 3 (p. 166)

1. While I was taking a shower, a mouse ran across my bathroom floor.

2. Sitting on the front porch, we were annoyed by mosquitoes.

3. While Kareem was eating at the restaurant, his coat was stolen.

4. Breathing heavily, the runner finally saw the finish line come into view.

5. Hoping to catch a glimpse of the band, fans filled the parking lot.

16 PARALLELISM

Practice 1 (p. 175)

1. to print the final copy

2. baby cried

3. dark sunglasses

4. office manager

5. unkind

6. coaches the track team

Practice 2 (p. 175)

1. play the piano

2. steamed shrimp

3. high-heeled boots

4. friendliness

5. deposited it in the deep hole

Practice 3 (p. 176)

Note Answers will vary. Below are some possibilities.

1. my TV remote control

2. wait for sales

3. creative writing

4. plant flowers

5. reading newspapers

ANSWERS TO THE PRACTICES IN PART TWO

17 PAPER FORM

Practice (p. 186)

	Community Service in the 21st Century
	Soon after becoming president, Barack Obama urged
	Americans to follow his example and look for ways to serve
	their communities. Many people, inspired by his words, have
	volunteered in local and national programs. The idea is a
	good one for several reasons. . . .

18 SPELLING

Practice (p. 188)

1. parties
2. referred
3. writing
4. definitely
5. deceive
6. employer
7. admittance
8. marrying
9. friendly
10. pitiful

19 PRONOUN TYPES

Practice (p. 192)

1. your
2. hers
3. me
4. He, I
5. I
6. Those
7. Who
8. these
9. they, themselves
10. whom

20 ADJECTIVES AND ADVERBS

Practice (p. 195)

1. harder
2. regularly
3. really
4. greatest
5. easier
6. softly
7. less
8. carefully
9. well
10. better

21 NUMBERS AND ABBREVIATIONS

Practice (p. 198)

1. five
2. 25
3. company
4. One hundred fifty
5. college
6. 6
7. doctor
8. 7
9. professor
10. 10

22 USAGE

Practice (p. 199)

1. ~~can't hardly~~ can hardly
2. ~~try and~~ try to
3. ~~ways~~ way
4. ~~had ought~~ ought
5. ~~could of~~ could have
6. ~~should of~~ should have
7. ~~couldn't help but notice~~ couldn't help noticing
8. ~~Being that~~ Since (*or* Because)
9. ~~off of~~ off
10. ~~anywheres~~ anywhere

23 MIXED CONSTRUCTIONS

Practice (p. 202)

1. I got an A on the exam because I studied all my class notes.

   (*Or:* The reason I got an A on the exam is that I studied all my class notes.)
2. That dog is ten years old, but he still runs around like a puppy.

   (*Or:* Although that dog is ten years old, he still runs around like a puppy.)
3. Eating healthy foods and reducing portion sizes helped me lose twenty pounds.

   (*Or:* By eating healthy foods and reducing portion sizes, I was able to lose twenty pounds.)
4. A recent immigrant's application for citizenship can take a long time.

   (*Or:* When a recent immigrant applies for citizenship, the process can take a long time.)
5. People who live alone often become depressed during the holiday season.

   (*Or:* For people who live alone, the holiday season is often depressing.)
6. Revision is a process in which a writer improves a paper by finalizing details, organizing clearly, and correcting spelling and grammar.

   (*Or:* During revision, a writer improves a paper by finalizing details, organizing clearly, and correcting spelling and grammar.)
7. Because Kaylin set a new track record at her high school, she was offered a scholarship.

   (*Or:* Kaylin set a new track record at her high school; therefore, she was offered a scholarship.)
8. At the beginning of the year, students register for classes.

   (*Or:* The beginning of the year is the time when students register for classes.)

24 MORE ABOUT SUBJECTS AND VERBS

Practice (p. 203)

1. *Subjects:* mitt, skateboard, pile
   Verb: belong
2. *Subject:* motor
   Verbs: coughed, refused
3. *Subjects:* Accounting, computer science
   Verbs: are, require
4. *Subject:* Lisa
   Verbs: tore, lifted, gasped

5. *Subjects:* author, husband
    Verbs: attended, sipped, chatted

25   EVEN MORE ABOUT VERBS

Practice 1 (p. 205)

1. Seeing . . . believing
2. to grow
3. has given
4. will be traveling . . . will be displaying
5. was borrowed

Practice 2 (p. 207)

1. sit
2. lain
3. raise
4. rose
5. laid

26   MORE ABOUT SUBJECT-VERB AGREEMENT

Practice (p. 208)

1. *Subject:* few
    Verb: taste
2. *Subjects:* Thelma, mother
    Verb: stays
3. *Subjects:* Carl, friends
    Verb: are
4. *Subject:* All
    Verb: were
5. *Subjects:* coach, coaches
    Verb: have
6. *Subject:* Both
    Verb: need
7. *Subjects:* lectures, textbook
    Verb: has
8. *Subject:* any
    Verb: Is
9. *Subject:* any
    Verb: Are
10. *Subject:* all
    Verb: seem

27   MORE ABOUT RUN-ONS AND COMMA SPLICES

Practice (p. 211)

1. horrible;
2. money;
3. locked;
4. London;
5. products;
6. rent;
7. children;
8. yard;
9. minutes;
10. much;

28   MORE ABOUT THE COMMA

Practice 1 (p. 214)

1. Vanessa,
2. morning,
3. March 8, 2010, Courthouse, Streets, Glendale,
4. confused,
5. no commas needed
6. Harvey, Joy,
7. No,
8. reception,
9. loan,
10. Rhett, . . . With love,

Practice 2 (p. 215)

1. bed,
2. see,
3. Delia,
4. graduate,
5. see,

29   MORE ABOUT THE APOSTROPHE

Practice (p. 216)

1. T's
2. no apostrophes needed
3. A's . . . B's
4. no apostrophes needed
5. *please's . . . thank-you's*

30   MORE ABOUT QUOTATION MARKS

Practice (p. 218)

1. "For our next class, please read the short story 'The Yellow Wallpaper' and write a journal entry about it," the instructor said.
2. "I can't believe it—they just scored the winning basket with half a second remaining!" the announcer gasped.
3. In which of Shakespeare's plays does a character say, "To thine own self be true"?
4. One of the longest words in the English language is "antidisestablishmentarianism."
5. "Whenever I'm feeling depressed, my father always makes me smile by saying, 'Life is far too important to be taken seriously,'" Joanne said.

31   MORE ABOUT PUNCTUATION MARKS

Practice (p. 220)

1. thirty-nine
2. food—
3. Reader's Digest . . . epidemic; . . . office;
4. (1) . . . (2) . . . (3) . . . (4) . . . (5) . . . (6)
5. The Tommyknockers . . . The Fly

32   MORE ABOUT CAPITAL LETTERS

Practice (p. 221)

1. Korean War . . . CIA
2. Northeast . . . Midwest
3. AIDS . . . Dark Ages
4. PBS
5. Dear Sir . . . Madam . . . DVD . . . Yours

33   MORE ABOUT HOMONYMS

Practice (p. 225)

1. already . . . quit . . . accept . . . advice
2. dessert . . . effect . . . dose
3. lose . . . less . . . an . . . pair . . . a
4. desert . . . loose . . . coarse
5. all ready . . . Fewer
6. quite . . . quit . . . advise . . . affect
7. desert . . . except
8. course . . . principle . . . among
9. quiet . . . does
10. where . . . were . . . led . . . among

34   MORE ABOUT WORD CHOICE

Practice (p. 226)

1. ~~remit~~ pay
   ~~prior to~~ before
2. ~~ascertained~~ found out
   ~~depart~~ leave
3. ~~remuneration~~ pay
   ~~insufficient~~ too low
4. ~~vociferous~~ noisy
   ~~endeavored~~ tried
5. ~~Subsequent to~~ After
   ~~inundating~~ flooding
6. ~~commenced~~ began
   ~~be victorious~~ win
7. ~~justifications~~ excuses
   ~~prevaricated~~ lied
8. ~~replenish~~ refill
   ~~deplete~~ empty
9. ~~domicile~~ home
   ~~transmit~~ send
10. ~~delectable~~ delicious
    ~~repast~~ meal

Index